Making sense of
ENGLISH

Bill Lucas with Brian Keaney

Oxford University Press 1987

To the teacher

This book is designed so that teachers in school may reproduce certain individual pages for classroom use *without* obtaining the prior permission of Oxford University Press.

This applies to the following pages **only**:
Pages 6; 31; 43; 45; 85; 125; 126.

Permission to reproduce any other part of this book must be requested from Oxford University Press.

Oxford University Press, Walton Street, Oxford OX2 6DP

Oxford New York Toronto
Delhi Bombay Calcutta Madras Karachi
Petaling Jaya Singapore Hong Kong Tokyo
Nairobi Dar es Salaam Cape Town
Melbourne Auckland

and associated companies in
Beirut Berlin Ibadan Nicosia

Oxford is a trade mark *of Oxford University Press*

© Oxford University Press 1987

ISBN 0 19 833166 7

Set by Tradespools Ltd, Frome, Somerset
Printed in Great Britain by Scotprint, Edinburgh

Contents

Introduction

To the student

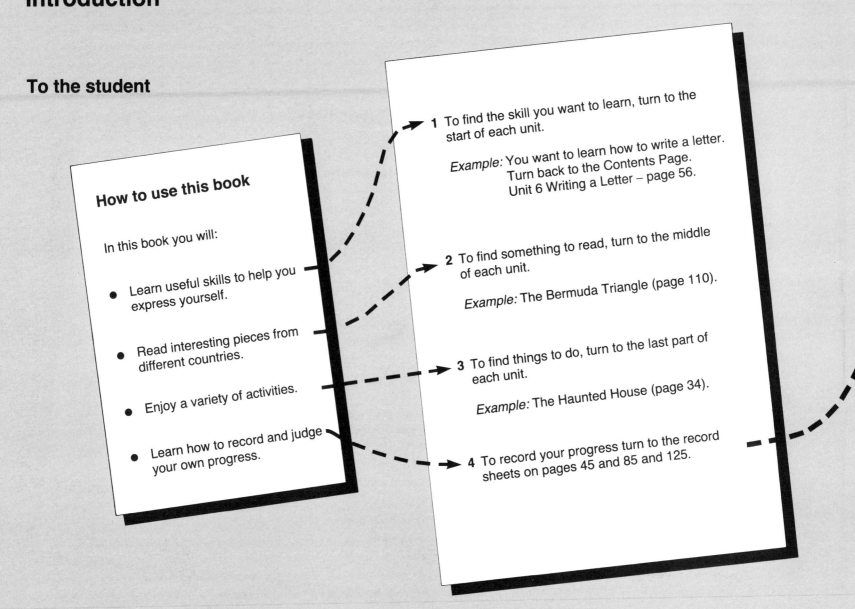

How to use this book

In this book you will:

- Learn useful skills to help you express yourself.

- Read interesting pieces from different countries.

- Enjoy a variety of activities.

- Learn how to record and judge your own progress.

1 To find the skill you want to learn, turn to the start of each unit.

Example: You want to learn how to write a letter.
Turn back to the Contents Page.
Unit 6 Writing a Letter – page 56.

2 To find something to read, turn to the middle of each unit.

Example: The Bermuda Triangle (page 110).

3 To find things to do, turn to the last part of each unit.

Example: The Haunted House (page 34).

4 To record your progress turn to the record sheets on pages 45 and 85 and 125.

How to fill in the record sheets

Read this page carefully before you try to fill anything in on the record sheets.

1 Each time you use the record sheets write in a different colour and record the date at the top. This way you will know *when* you learned to do something.

2 You can fill it in every week, every month, every term or as often as is convenient.
   Probably three or four times a term would be enough.

3 You may want to fill it in when you have just learned something or when you have been studying something for some time.
   Often skills take a long time to be really learned; so don't expect sudden results – keep practising.

4 You can fill a small part of it in when you start using this book.
   You will probably leave most of it blank.

5 You can fill it in when your teacher suggests you are beginning to learn something or when you have learned it.

6 You can just tick under the right face
   or add a comment of your own
   or do both.

7 You can see your progress as you record over a period of time.

8 You can ask for help in areas where you don't feel so confident.

Note: Don't write on the pages in this book. Write on copies of these pages which your teacher will give you.

To the teacher

Various activities throughout the book are indicated by the symbols below:

Read

Write

Pair talk

Group talk

Read aloud

Tape record

Unit 1: Communicating experiences

Your experiences

1 Who is the first person you remember in your life apart from your family?
....

2 What is the first place you can remember? ....

Why? ....

3 What is the happiest thing you can recall from early childhood? ....

.... Recently? ....

4 Have you ever been frightened? ....

When? ....

5 What is the most exciting thing that has happened to you at school?

....

6 Have you ever made a fool of yourself? ....

When? ....

7 Have you ever been punished for something you did not do? ....

Explain. ....

8 Have you ever wished that you had behaved in a different way? ....

Give an example. ....

9 Have you ever done something you knew was wrong? ....

10 Have you ever been hurt? ....

11 Have you ever hurt anyone? ....

12 If you had to describe one experience in your life so far what would it be?

.... Why? ....

13 Make a list of five important things that have happened to you in:
a) the last year
b) the last week
c) the last few hours.
Example:

> The last year.
> 1. I changed schools.
> 2. I fell in love.
> 3. I played for the school football team.
> 4. . . . .

14 Using the questions on the other side of this page or the list you have just made, choose something that has happened to you recently. Write down anything that comes into your mind about the experience. Include any interesting details you can remember.
Example:

My birthday

What happened   My family forgot
                                          How I felt

THE DAY I RAN AWAY FROM HOME

Phoned home and
reversed the charges
                          Cycled 20 miles   Took money from
                          to Dublin   Mum's purse on
                                               kitchen shelf

15 Using your notes to help you, talk about your experience. Try to make it as interesting and lively as you can.

Other people's experiences

Writing about personal experiences is like talking about them, except that you need to be more organised.

Free dinners

Lorraine was in my first-year class at school and the only reason I noticed her was because she was on free dinners like me. We was the only two in that class who had to take the shame of it. We had a right nasty teacher, Mr Cobb, (so you know what we used to call him). Just the way he called your name at the end of the register made you crawl and feel two feet small. He'd collect the money from the other kids and make Lorraine and me queue up separately at his table. Not that he ever said anything to us. He just finished with the regular kids and then announced 'Free Dinners' even though there was only two of us.

by *Farrukh Dhondy*

1 What experiences are being described by Farrukh Dhondy?
2 Why do you think the writer chose them?
3 What makes this sound like someone *talking* about an experience?
4 Have you ever had similar feelings? If so, explain.

Talking blues

The other day I was walking on Canterbury Road and I saw my little cousin and him have a five-speed bicycle. And I look and I tell him, well, I did want to borrow him bicycle to go somewhere. So him give me the bicycle. So I got on the bicycle, I was on the bicycle, and I was riding up pass the police station ready to go on the road. A police walk out, like him never have nothing to do, so him call I, and I being innocent didn't run or anything, I just went to him. And him say: 'How come a black man is riding a five-speed bicycle?' And I ask him what him mean by that? And him say: 'If a black man ride a no-gear bicycle, is nothing, but when you see black people riding five gear and driving cars, well something is wrong because we don't like to see that'. That is what the policeman say to I.

So same time I say is my brother bicycle. Him say, 'No, you steal that bike'. And I say: 'What you mean I steal that bike? There is me cousin down there, I will go and call him'. And same time him grab me in me collar and say, 'No you coming in here with me'. So I say: 'What am I coming in here for?' And him say: 'You nick that bicycle'. And I say I can prove that I didn't nick it. And him pull me, and a next two come out, and dem draw me in the police station.

from *Affor*

G

How do you react to this? Was it fair? What would you have been thinking if you were:
  a) the man on the bicycle
  b) his cousin
  c) the policeman?

Families

In this passage a woman remembers a number of experiences from her childhood.

I can still remember that when my father used to go out to work during the day, my mother used to come to us and speak to us through the key hole and ask how we were treated by my father and whether we were hungry or not. After a few months my father couldn't cope with looking after us single-handed while having to work for us day and night. One day my twin sister Fatima had fallen down the stairs; at the bottom of the stairs there was a thin window and she went right through it, and ended up falling two storeys. This was while my father was at work and there was nobody looking after us. Fatima was rushed to the hospital by our neighbours, because she was lying in a pool of blood that was gushing out from her forehead. Everybody thought that she was going to die, but, thank God, she survived this dreadful accident.

While she was in hospital I had a little accident as well. One day I made my brother Hassan very angry, because I made my father beat him with a thick leather belt for being naughty while my father was at work. Hassan kept on crying and the tears kept running down his cheeks while his eyes were fixed on my face waiting for a chance to get hold of me and cool his anger. The following day when my father went out to work, I realised that it was a good opportunity for Hassan to fulfil his promise and obviously I was scared stiff at that moment. My knees kept on knocking against each other, because I knew that there wasn't anybody around to defend me, so I ran up the wooden staircase to reach the attic and lock myself in until my father returned. But unfortunately he was standing near the kitchen door, holding the handle. The handle wasn't properly fixed to the door and so it came away in his hand. While I was climbing the stairs in a great hurry, I turned around to see whether he was after me or not. He threw the handle at me and it got stuck to the left side of my forehead like a pin stuck in a pincushion. Obviously the blood kept on rushing out of the wound and Hassan was puzzled for a moment and did not know what to do. Then he ran out and vanished from my sight.

I had a white dress on with pink flowers: it was my favourite and that is why I can still remember it. It was nearly covered in blood. I was half-way on the stairs when I felt completely weak and feeble in the knees and I think I must have fainted because I don't remember who took me to hospital or how they got the handle out. All I can remember was lying in a glaring white bed next to Fatima who looked so cheerful. I felt my head and it was covered with bandages and there was this awful pain across my head, and a very kind nurse dressed up all in white came to me with a cheerful smile on her face and helped me sit up and gave me some medicine which tasted like syrup – I loved it.

I stayed in the hospital for a few months and then left it with a scar on the left side of my forehead. Both my sister and I left the hospital at the same time and both of us had a scar on our foreheads; she had it in the middle of her forehead. This incident took place in 1966 when I was only five years old, and after the divorce of my parents.

by *Zohra El Kssmi*

1 Make a list of the different experiences described by Zohra El Kssmi.
2 Which details in this piece make her memories come alive?

8

Refugees

We were to travel in the 'Zanzibar', but we were not the only ones. The dockyards were crowded with people – all Indians: there were the Sikhs with turbans and British clothes (oily trousers and flip-flops); there were the excited traders and the railway workers, and beside the beggars and porters, among all the other noisy, long-legged, skinny young men, was I. My uncle stood beside me. He looked anxious. Meanwhile, I was confused and gaped at the sight of so many people – people of all sizes and ages. It was incredible that there were so many people in so small an area, not forgetting the luggage which was packed in large strong metal trunks. They were travelling with their life's collection of odds and ends. Some carried heavy mattresses on their backs and I could hear their cooking utensils clanging inside their loads.

by *Sabir Bandali*

➡ Using the picture and the passage to help you, try to imagine how *you* would feel if you were leaving your country to start a new life. Write down your thoughts.

The envelope

Another powerful feeling felt by many people at some stage in their lives is failure. Read this description of how it feels.

I picked up the envelope addressed in my own handwriting and knew what the horrible thing contained and stood staring at it, like a rabbit hypnotized by a snake...

'For heaven's sake get on with it and stop dithering about like an old hen,' growled my father, slicing the top off his boiled egg with millimetric accuracy.

Now don't get me wrong. I'm not scared of my dad. He's a great guy. Besides I've grown used to him. It's just that he's too much, if you know what I mean. He walks into a room and it's crowded.

I opened the envelope. It split all ways and the contents fluttered to the floor. I managed to get at them first, dad being occupied with his runny yolk at the time.

So I read my results. I thought they'd be bad. They were worse. Silently I handed them over.

'It doesn't seem much to go out in the world with,' he remarked gently. 'One CSE grade four in Metalwork.'

by *Gene Kemp*

 1 Which part of this description stands out most when reading it?

 2 Imagine you have just received these results. Talk about your feelings at that moment.

Different kinds of personal experience

In this unit we have looked at some different kinds of personal experience, but there are many others.

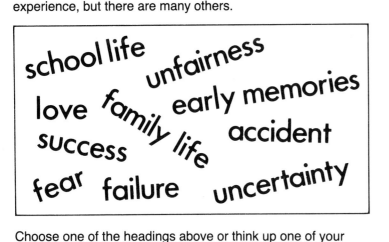

school life unfairness
love family early memories
success life accident
fear failure uncertainty

Choose one of the headings above or think up one of your own. Write down all your feelings and ideas about this area of your experience. Organise these into sections like the passages you have read.

Under attack

As I walked up the street I felt as if a big spotlight was on me but I kept walking, up to that frightening line of silent men. Then something hit the road just by my feet. It was a half-brick! I actually looked up at the sky, as if it had fallen from the clouds or something, and then another one whizzed past my ear and it dawned on me that someone in the crowd was chucking them at me.

'Hey,' I shouted. 'Hey, listen, . . .

by *Peter Carter*

This is the beginning of someone else's experience. Imagine you are him. Continue the story as it might have gone on.

The market

Read aloud these two accounts of the same experience.

A I went down the market – right – to get some fruit. I had this list – apples, bananas and some vegetables as well. I looked around the stalls and I found this one that was selling green peppers dead cheap. So I went there. I had to queue for ages. In the end she served me. She sort of started getting my apples before she had finished giving the woman in front her change. I got a few different things – I can't remember everything. And it came to eighty something pence. So I gave her a pound. She gave me the change and it didn't look like enough to me. I was going to say something but she'd started on the next person straight away. Anyway I went round to the front of the stall to look at the prices and work it out. Then I realised that she had given me the wrong change, right. Not only that but she'd overcharged me in the first place. So I went back and said excuse me I think you've charged me too much. Well you should have seen her. She went all right any one can make a mistake really loud. I said I wasn't having a go. She said it's just your attitude. Well that was ridiculous because I was dead calm. I mean anyone can make a mistake, that's true. There's no need to go mad. She said. What's the matter? I started to explain but she couldn't take it in. She said look how much do I owe you? She was getting all worked up. She kept shouting how much do I owe you then. I started getting confused myself so I said forty pence. She handed me forty pence and I went off. Afterwards I worked out she only owed me twenty one pence.

B I went to the market to buy some fruit and vegetables. I found a stall that was selling green peppers cheaply and I queued up. The woman began to serve me before she had finished giving the last customer her change. That might have been what made her give me too little change. I wasn't certain at first. Then I went round and checked on the prices at the front of the stall. I saw that she'd also charged me too much in the first place. I went back and said quite calmly, 'Excuse me, I think you've charged me too much.'

She completely over-reacted. 'All right,' she shouted. 'Anyone can make a mistake.'

I said, 'I'm not having a go.'

'It's just your attitude,' she replied. That was ridiculous because I was being very polite. But I didn't let her annoy me. I just began to explain her mistake.

Instead of listening she started shouting, 'How much do I owe you then? How much do I owe you?'

I got confused myself and said, 'Forty pence.'

She put her hand in her money bag, took out the forty pence and thrust it at me as if she would have liked to choke me with it. I just walked away.

Afterwards I totalled it up. She'd only owed me twenty-one pence. What a shame!

G

1 Which of these two examples sounds as if someone is **talking** about an experience?
   a) *Passage A* She went all right anyone can make a mistake really loud.
   b) *Passage B* 'All right,' she shouted. 'Anyone can make a mistake.'
Can you decide why?

2 Which words are normally used when *talking* about experiences? (Example: *sort of.*)

3 Choose other examples from the two passages. Write them down and compare them.

4 Why do you think the woman started shouting?

5 Describe the experiences that the customer went through and why it was upsetting.

6 How old do you think the customer was?

7 Which passage is best at bringing the experience alive? Why?

Choose something which has happened to you recently. It could be an embarrassing experience like the one you have just read about, or something that has happened at home or at school.

P

In pairs, describe it to each other and then write about it. Compare what you hear with what you read.

➡

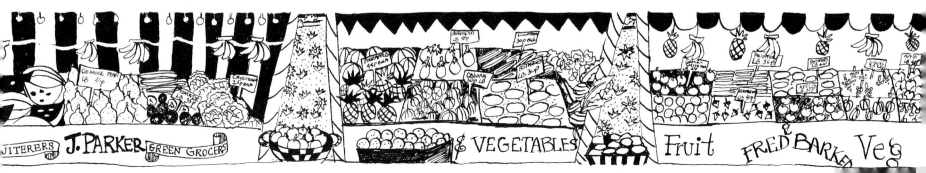

Hark, hark the dogs do bark

by *Janet Frame*

One morning, during my first week at school, I sneaked into Mum and Dad's bedroom, opened the top drawer of the chest, where the coins 'brought back from the war' were kept, and helped myself to a handful. I then went to Dad's best trousers hanging behind the door, put my hand in the pocket (how cold and slippery the lining!), and took out two coins. Hearing someone coming, I hastily thrust the money under the chest and left the room, and later, when the coast was clear, I retrieved my hoard and on my way to school stopped at Heath's store to buy some chewing gum.

Mr Heath looked sternly at me. 'This money won't buy anything,' he said. 'It's Egyptian.'

'I know,' I lied. Then, handing him the money from Dad's pocket, I asked, 'Will this buy me some chewing gum?'

'That's better,' he said, returning yet another of the coins, a farthing.

Armed with a supply of chewing gum, I waited at the door of the Infant Room, a large room with a platform or stage at one end and double doors opening on to Standard One, and as the children went into the room, I gave each a 'pillow' of chewing gum. Later, Miss Botting, a woman in a blue costume the same colour as the <u>castor-oil</u> bottle, suddenly stopped her teaching and asked, 'Billy Delamare, what are you eating?'

'Chewing gum, Miss Botting.'

'Where did you get it?'

'From Jean Frame, Miss Botting.' (I was known at school as Jean and at home as Nini.)

'Dids McIvor, where did you get your chewing gum?'

'From Jean Frame, Miss.'

'Jean Frame, where did you get the chewing gum?'

'From Heath's, Miss Botting.'

'Where did you get the money?'

'My father gave it to me.'

Evidently Miss Botting did not believe me. Suddenly she was <u>determined</u> to get 'the truth' out of me. She repeated her question. 'Where did you get the money? I want the *truth*.'

I repeated my answer, changing *Dad* for *father*.

'Come out here.'

I came out in front of the class.

'Go up on the platform.'

I went up on to the platform.

'Now tell me where you got the money.'

I repeated my answer.

Playtime came. The rest of the class went out to play while Miss Botting and I grimly faced each other.

'Tell me the truth,' she said.

I replied, 'Dad gave me the money.'

She sent for Myrtle and Bruddie, who informed her with piping innocence that Dad did not give me the money.

'Yes, he did,' I insisted. 'He called me back when you had both gone to school.'

'He didn't.'

'He did.'

All morning I stayed on the platform. The class continued their reading lessons. I stayed on the platform through lunchtime and into the afternoon, still refusing to confess. I was beginning to feel afraid, instead of defiant, as if I hadn't a friend in the world, and because I knew that Myrtle and Bruddie would 'tell' as soon as they got home, I felt that I never wanted to go home. All the places I had found – the birch log in Glenham, the top of the climbers in Edendale, the places in the songs and poems – seemed to have vanished, leaving me with no place. I held out obstinately until mid-afternoon, when the light was growing thin with masses of dark tiredness showing behind it, and the schoolroom was filled with a nowhere dust, and a small voice answered from the scared me in answer to Miss Botting's repeated question. 'I took the money out of my father's pocket.'

While I'd been lying, I had somehow protected myself; I knew now that I had no protection. I'd been found out as a thief. I was so appalled by my future prospects that I don't remember if Miss Botting strapped me. I know she gave the news to the class, and it spread quickly around the school that I was a thief. Loitering at the school gate, wondering where to go and what to do, I saw Myrtle and Bruddie, carefree as ever, on their way home. I walked slowly along the road. I don't know when I had learned to read, but I had read and knew the stories in the primer books, and I thought of the story of the fox that sprang out from the side of the road and swallowed the child. No one knew what had happened or where the child had gone, until one day when the fox was walking by, a kind person heard, 'Let me out, let me out!' coming from the fox's belly, at which the kind person killed the fox, slit the belly open, and lo, the child emerged whole, unharmed, and was taken by the kind person to live in a wood in a cottage made of coconut ice with a licorice chimney . . .

I finally arrived at our place. Myrtle was leaning over the gate. 'Dad knows,' she said, in a matter-of-fact voice. I went up the path. The front door was open and Dad was waiting with the strap in his hand. 'Come into the bedroom,' he said sternly. He gave me his usual 'hiding,' not excessive, as some children had, but sharp and full of anger that one of his children was a *thief. Thief, thief.* At home and at school I was now called *Thief.*

1 Look up the underlined words in the dictionary on page 126. (If you don't know how to use it, turn to Unit 11, page 107.)

2 Imagine you are Jean Frame. Choose one of these ideas:
   a) continue the story describing how you felt after being beaten by your father,
   b) write out the conversation that you might have had with:
      – Miss Botting . . . next time you saw her
      – Your father . . . next morning at breakfast

Talk about your reactions to what Jean did and how you would have felt.

Sign of the times

1 Look at these sign-posts. What do they mean to you?

In fact they are road signs warning of:
a) an accident
b) a steep hill down
c) an uneven road.

2 Look at the stories and extracts you have read in this unit. In pairs, decide which of these signs could apply to experiences that *people* have as well as cars.
Example: 'Families' on page 8 could have the 'accident' sign-post. Decide why.
If you think these three signs don't fit the experiences described so far in the book make up your own.

3 Think of experiences that these signs could describe.

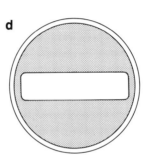

4 Make up signs of your own to fit the three shapes below.

a) These warn you of something that is going to happen.
b) These tell you *not to do* something.
c) These tell you *to do* something.

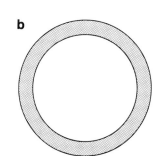

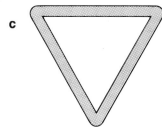

5 In pairs, talk about your life so far. You could include:
   - where and when you were born
   - your early memories
   - your family
   - your schools
   - important things that happened to you
   - moments when you have had to take decisions
   - times when other people have decided things about you
   - things you wish you hadn't done.

6 Ask your partner to pick one experience from what you have described and make up a sign for this experience and write a paragraph next to it explaining:
   a) why you have chosen the sign
   b) what the experience meant to you.

7 Use sign-posts to describe your whole life so far.

   Example: If you were Mohammed Ali they could be –

GIVE WAY

ACCIDENT

8 Make up sign-posts for other famous people.

Unit 2: Using sentences

What is a sentence?

> A sentence starts with a capital letter and ends with a full stop. It must make complete sense.

A

> about Advertisement
> saw an new television
> game yesterday

B

> Yesterday I saw an
> advertisement about a
> new television game.

Make a list of all the differences between the two examples.
This is how you could start:

> 1. B ends in a full stop
> 2. In A there are words missed out
> 3.
> 4.

Example B is called a sentence.

Using a sentence chart

1 Copy the chart below, but leave enough space to do some more examples. If you find a sentence write YES in the last box.

  C Paul found a five-pound note on Monday.
  D Five pound note on Monday.
  E a new television game.
  F yesterday I saw a great new game.
  G Hull United are at the top of the first division.
  H chewing gum.
  I My dad always chews gum.
  J we have a dog called 'Lamp-post'

2 Make up five more examples yourself and fill in the chart for each one.

Ex	Does it make sense?	Is anything missed out?	Capital Letter?	Full Stop?	What is it about?	?
A	X	✓	X	X	Impossible to know	NO
B	✓	X	✓	✓	T.V. Game	YES
C						

The Hotel Marina has a large, modern swimming pool.

This attractive, modern hotel is five minutes from the beach.

Holidays

Look at the two pictures above:

> The words below the pictures are sentences.

➡ Imagine you are a travel agent. You have been sent these two photographs to display on the wall. Think up a sentence for each one and write it down.

Design a holiday picture and make up a sentence for it.

Giving opinions

Often the words we write or say are what we **think** about something. This is called giving an opinion.

1 Make a list of five sentences about things you like and five about things you hate:
Example:

1. I like going on holiday. 2. 3.	1. I hate.... 2. 3.

Here is another example:
  I like the feel of mud between my toes because it is warm and slimey.

2 Make sentences for these pictures using these words to help you.

Patience

by *Brian Keaney*

Terry Ford was the meanest person Jackie had ever met. He worked with Jackie's dad. You should have heard her dad complain about him:

'Tight!' he used to say. 'That Terry Ford is as tight as an elastic band round an elephant!'

That was why Jackie was so shocked when she heard about Terry's offer of a lift. Everyone was. Jackie's dad was as surprised as anybody else.

'I can't understand it,' he said, 'but I'd be a fool to turn it down.'

'Just a minute,' my mum said. 'Let me get this right. Terry Ford has offered to drive us down to the caravan next weekend for nothing. Is that what you're telling me?'

My dad nodded. 'I know,' he said. 'I can't believe it myself.'

'There's a catch in this,' Jackie thought.

The caravan was on a site near Clacton. They were hiring it from Mr Bettis who ran the local shop. Jackie wasn't sure whether she was looking forward to it or not. It was better than no holiday at all, she reckoned. But ten days cooped up in a caravan with her mum and dad and her sister, Chris, didn't exactly sound like a barrel of laughs.

She was right. It wasn't a barrel of laughs. She was right about Terry Ford as well: there was a catch. He turned up on Saturday morning, sure enough, and they all squeezed into his battered Volkswagen. It was pretty cramped but no one was complaining. After a couple of hours on the motorway Jackie was wishing that they'd gone by train. But her mum and dad were in a good mood and that was worth something. Normally long journeys meant that her old man got really niggly and ready to bite your head off. This time he was in a really good mood. He stopped off when they got into Clacton and bought half a dozen cans of lager. Then they finally reached the caravan site and he sat there outside the caravan with Terry drinking lager out of the can while Mum, Jackie and Chris unloaded all the luggage.

It must have been about midday when they arrived. Jackie and Chris went down to the beach. It was great. They lay about in the sun, messed about burying each other in the sand. Chris even had a dip in the water but it was freezing. It was getting on for seven o'clock when they got back after having a go on the amusements. Jackie was very surprised to see Terry Ford still there. Her mum and dad didn't look so cheerful any more.

'Mum,' she whispered, the first time she got a chance, 'when's he going?'

'I don't know,' she whispered back. She had a worried look on her face. Suddenly Jackie had a sinking feeling in her stomach. She looked at Terry. He was sitting at the table reading a newspaper.

'We've been lumbered,' Jackie thought to herself, 'well and truly lumbered.'

Jackie's mum said they couldn't say anything to him that night because he had just driven all the way from London. So Terry slept in one of the bedrooms. Jackie's mum and dad slept in the other. She and Chris had to sleep on the floor in the kitchen.

'I expect he'll be off early tomorrow,' Mum said.

'Oh yeah?' Jackie thought.

The next day was just the same. He sat there playing patience with a deck of cards that he found in a drawer in the caravan. Jackie felt like hitting him with something.

Finally her mum told her and Chris to go off to the

us and he couldn't go back now because he'd got somebody staying in his house for the week.'

'You're joking!'

'Of course I'm not joking,' her mother snapped.

'But dad didn't invite him, did he?' Jackie went on. Her mother shrugged.

'I suppose he could have misunderstood,' she said.

'But Mum, we can't just let him stay.'

'What else can we do?'

*

Jackie was all for throwing him out but her parents just weren't like that. They were stuck with Terry Ford. He didn't seem bothered. He just sat there smiling to himself and playing patience. He didn't even go out anywhere. In the end they all took to going out as often as possible just to get away from him. The worst days were when it rained. Jackie and Chris went and hung around in the amusement arcades. The atmosphere was terrible in that caravan, especially with Jackie and Chris sleeping on the floor every night. When the day finally arrived for them to go home it was like being let out of prison.

Mum and Dad were up with the dawn, practically. They had everything ready while Terry was still in his pyjamas. Terry had a lengthy breakfast and took ages to get packed but at last he was ready. Everyone got into the car in silence.

The journey home was awful. Just outside London they ran out of petrol. They just managed to limp into a garage. Terry kept muttering about not being able to understand it and being sure he'd calculated the right amount. Anyway he had to put some in and would you believe it? He didn't have enough money. Jackie's dad had to lend him a pound. You should have heard him swearing. But he paid up. He had to.

beach. She could tell from the way she said it that there was going to be some sort of showdown. Her dad was moving about on his chair as if he had worms. So Jackie didn't say a word. She just took off and Chris followed her. Somehow they couldn't enjoy themselves on the beach, though. They were on edge, waiting for the result. They were just thinking about going back when their mum came walking along the beach towards them.

'What happened, Mum?' Jackie asked.

'Your dad asked Terry when he was going home,' she said.

'And...?'

She looked at the beach and shrugged.

'What did he say, Mum?' Jackie insisted.

'He said that your dad had invited him along with

When they got back Terry insisted on stopping at his house first. He made a big fuss about stopping off to pay Jackie's dad the pound he owed him for the petrol.

'No one can call me mean,' he said. 'No one can say that Terry Ford doesn't pay his way.'

Nobody answered him. There didn't seem to be any point. Terry pulled up right outside his house and got out of the car.

'Right,' he said. 'Just you wait here.'

They sat in the car fuming. Five minutes passed.

'He's an awful long time,' Jackie's mum said.

'Why don't we get out and walk?' Jackie asked.

Just then Terry Ford reappeared. He looked white and shaken. He staggered over to the car.

'Whatever's the matter?' Jackie's mum asked.

Terry looked as if he could hardly speak. Finally he croaked out. 'It's the house. It's been burgled.'

'Burgled?' said Jackie's dad. 'But I thought you had someone staying here.'

Terry looked down at the ground. He mumbled something.

'What was that?' Jackie's dad replied. 'Speak up.'

'I was lying,' Terry admitted.

Jackie tried not to laugh but she couldn't help it. The laughter happened of its own accord. In a moment Jackie's mum and dad joined in. Terry just stood there looking pathetic. 'I'm glad you think it's funny,' he said at last.

'I'm sorry,' Jackie's dad said, recovering himself. 'Never mind Terry. I expect you'll get it all back on the insurance. You are insured aren't you?' he added.

Terry looked as if salt had been rubbed into his wounds.

'Oh Terry,' Jackie's dad said. 'You don't mean...'

Terry nodded. 'I was going to,' he said. 'Only it seemed so expensive. I was going to, really I was.'

1 Now look at these pictures:

Terry Ford offers the family a lift.

The family get into Terry's car.

2 Here are some more pictures from the story. Make up sentences for each one like the ones above. (Turn back to page 16 to remind yourself what a sentence is.)

a  **b**

c

d

e

f

3 Here is the first part of Brian Keaney's story. There are some blank spaces in it. Copy it out and fill in the spaces. Sometimes you will need a full stop and sometimes a capital letter. When you have finished, turn back and see how much you got right.

___ erry Ford was the meanest person Jackie had ever met ___ He worked with Jackie's dad ___ You should have heard Jackie's dad complain about him:

'Tight!' he used to say. 'That Terry Ford is as tight as an elastic band round an elephant ___ ' ___ hat was why Jackie was so shocked when she heard about Terry's offer of a lift ___ Everyone was ___ Jackie's dad was as surprised as anybody else.

4 Look at this sentence taken from the story. The words on the left are jumbled up but on the right have been put back together. Make sentences out of these jumbled words taken from the story. The first one is done for you.
Example:

a was right He . → He was right.

b worked Jason's dad He with

c laughs It wasn't barrel a of

d great It was .

e Terry He looked at

f Terry Ford They stuck with were

5 These sentences have been left unfinished. Copy them out and use the story to help you finish them or make up endings yourself. <u>Remember to use a full stop.</u>
a) Terry Ford was the meanest _____
b) The caravan was _____
c) Jackie and Chris went down to _____
d) Terry Ford sat around playing _____
e) Just outside London _____
f) While he was on holiday, Terry's house in London _____
g) Jackie laughed _____
h) Terry's house wasn't insured because _____

Operation survival

Your school has a large hut in the country where groups can stay and live together. The hut is large enough for twelve people to sleep in it.

Here is a plan of the inside of the hut.

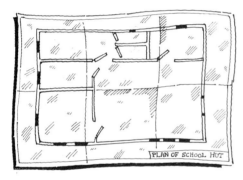

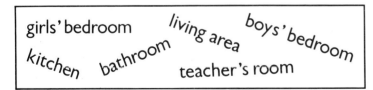

1 Copy this plan and label it. Imagine you are designing it for school groups to stay in – teachers and pupils. Here are some labels you could use. Think of your own if you want.

girls' bedroom   living area   boys' bedroom
kitchen   bathroom   teacher's room

You could also add beds, tables, basins, windows, or anything else you can think of.

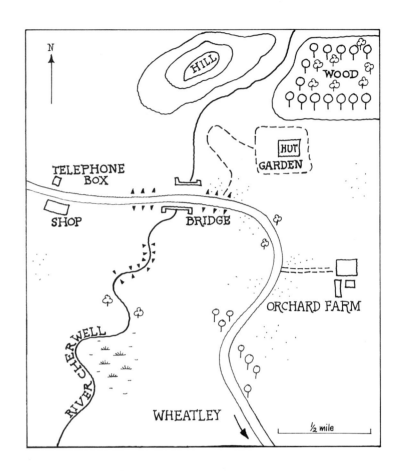

2 Look at this map. Find the hut. Make a list of all the things you can see on the map. Write them out as sentences. *Example:*

1. You get to the hut by a path
2. There is a ....
3.
4.
5.

Imagine you are on the last day of a three-day school trip to the hut. There are ten of you – nine and one teacher.
It is eight o'clock in the morning. Your teacher tunes to the local radio station and hears this:

```
... This is the eight o'clock news.  We have just
heard that a lorry carrying a dangerous chemical
has overturned in Wheatley.  The police say that
all people in this area must stay inside.  There
is a dangerous gas spreading over the area.  At
8.15 there will be more news ...
```

3 What does your teacher do?
What does she or he say to you?
Talk about this in pairs. Decide what you would do if you were the teacher.

You are now waiting for the next news flash. This is what you hear:

```
... After the news of the crashed chemical lorry
in Wheatley, here is more advice from the police.
Don't leave your house except in an emergency.
Shut all your doors and windows.  Keep your
radio on.  Turn off your gas.  Fill up your bath
with cold water.  If you need help, ring this
number, 010101 ...
```

4 Some of this advice is more important than the rest.
Decide which you think is the most important. Write down a list in order of importance. Put the most useful item at the top of your list.

5 How do you feel now? You had planned to pack up this morning and now you are stuck.
Talk about what *you* would do. You could work in a group. You have now had breakfast and are sitting in the living area. (Look back at the plan of the hut.)

6 Decide how you will pass the time until the next news flash. In the pictures below there are some ideas. Decide which ones you think are good and which you think are bad. Remember what the newsreader said.

7 Write down five good ideas of things to do.
Make up five sentences.
Set it out like the example.

FIVE THINGS I WOULD DO...

1. I would shut all the windows.

2.

3.

4.

5.

 The next news flash:

... and now more on the chemical accident.
Police say it may be twenty-four hours before it
is safe to go outside if you live in the Wheatley
area. Ring this number - 378214 - or dial 999
if you need help. Stay calm and don't panic. We
will give you more information as soon as we have
it ...

One of your group says she has terrible stomach pain. Your teacher thinks she needs a doctor. Someone must telephone the number given on the news. There's no phone in the hut. Who will go?

8 Look at the map again. Decide who will go and how to get to the phone-box. What would she or he wear?
Talk about who you would pick from your class and why.
Say if *you* would go or not.

9 Imagine you have decided to be the one to make the phone call. Here is how the call might go. Copy the conversation and fill in the gaps. You could work in pairs.

You: Hello! Is that the police?

Police: Yes. Who are you and where are you calling from?

You: My name is _____ .
    I am _____
    _____
    _____ .

Police: What are you doing there?
You: _____ .

Police: What is your problem?
You: _____ .

Police: We'll send a police helicopter as soon as possible.
You: _____ .

Police: Go straight back to your hut. Tell your teacher help is on its way. Stay calm!

Meanwhile . . .
Back at the hut everybody is hungry. This is all the food that's left in the kitchen:

10 Write down what you would do with this food. Compare your ideas with other people's.
This is how the one o'clock news starts:

```
... Police have just received a telephone call
from a party of school children.  They are
staying close to Orchard Farm, near Wheatley ....
..............................................
..............................................
..............................................
```

11 Copy this news flash and finish it off.

You are finally rescued and all get home safely. Your family ask for a step-by-step account of your amazing day.

12 Copy out this chart to help you remember what happened. For each time given, make up one or two sentences.

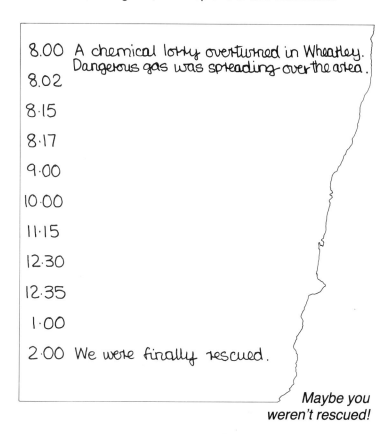

Time	
8.00	A chemical lorry overturned in Wheatley. Dangerous gas was spreading over the area.
8.02	
8.15	
8.17	
9.00	
10.00	
11.15	
12.30	
12.35	
1.00	
2.00	We were finally rescued.

Maybe you weren't rescued!

How else would you have liked this story to end? Talk about it together.

You could make a tape-recording of your group's opinions. You could use some of the news flashes. You could make a short radio programme on tape.

Unit 3: Understanding paragraphs

A The woman got up and walked to where the gentle surf washed over her ankles. The water was colder than the night air, for it was only mid-June. The woman called to her friend to join her but there was no answer from him. She backed up a few steps, then ran at the water. At first her strides were long and graceful, but then a small wave crashed into her knees. She just managed to remain standing and fling herself at the next tall wave. Then she began to swim with the jerky, head-above-water strokes of someone who has only recently learned how to. A hundred yards off shore, the shark sensed a change in the sea's rhythm. It did not see the woman, nor yet did it smell her. The fish turned towards the shore. The woman continued to swim away from the beach, stopping now and then to check her position by the lights shining from the house. The tide was slack, so she had not moved up or down the beach. But she was tiring, so she rested for a moment, treading water and then started for shore. The vibrations were stronger now and the fish recognised prey. The sweep of its tail quickened, thrusting the giant body forward. The woman felt only a wave of pressure as the fish closed on her. It seemed to lift her up in the water. She stopped swimming and held her breath. The fish smelled her now. It began to circle close to the surface. Its thrashing tail cut the glassy surface with a hiss. For the first time, the woman felt fear, though she did not know why. The fish was about forty feet away from the woman when it turned suddenly to the left and, with two quick thrusts of its tail, was upon her.

B The woman got up and walked to where the gentle surf washed over her ankles. The water was colder than the night air, for it was only mid-June. The woman called to her friend to join her in the sea, but there was no answer from him.

She backed up a few steps, then ran at the water. At first her strides were long and graceful, but then a small wave crashed into her knees. She just managed to remain standing and fling herself at the next tall wave. Then she began to swim with the jerky, head-above-water strokes of someone who has only recently learned how to.

A hundred yards off shore, the shark sensed a change in the sea's rhythm. It did not see the woman, nor yet did it smell her. The fish turned towards the shore.

The woman continued to swim away from the beach, stopping now and then to check her position by the lights shining from the house. The tide was slack, so she had not moved up or down the beach. But she was tiring, so she rested for a moment, treading water and then started for shore.

The vibrations were stronger now and the fish recognised prey. The sweeps of its tail quickened, thrusting the giant body forward.

The woman felt only a wave of pressure as the fish closed on her. It seemed to lift her up in the water. She stopped swimming and held her breath.

The fish smelled her now. It began to circle close to the surface. Its thrashing tail cut the glassy surface with a hiss.

For the first time, the woman felt fear, though she did not know why.

The fish was about forty feet away from the woman when it turned suddenly to the left and, with two quick thrusts of its tail, was upon her.

Adapted from *Jaws* by Peter Benchley

1 Make a list of what is the same and what is different in the two passages from *Jaws*. Which is easier to follow? Why?
Example:

Same	Different

Example **B** is easier to understand because the writing is divided up into smaller units. These are called paragraphs.

A paragraph is a group of sentences.
It starts on a new line.
It usually starts in from the margin.
It begins with a capital letter.
Each sentence ends with a full stop.

2 Look at this paragraph. Copy and complete the sentences in boxes.

A p___graph is a gr___ of s_____.

It starts in from the m_____.

The fish smelled her now. It began to circle close to the surface. Its thrashing tail cut the glassy surface with a hiss.

It begins with a c_____ letter.

Each sen_____ ends with a f___ s___.

3 Look at the first two paragraphs in Example B again. They are both about the woman. The first one is a group of sentences about the woman on the beach before she goes swimming. Decide what the second one is about.

4 Each of the nine paragraphs is either about the woman or about the shark. The last one is about both. Make a list and write the heading for each paragraph next to its number.
Example:

1. Woman on the beach.
2. Woman begins to....
3. . . . .

P

Here are some drawings to help you. Each one is a picture of one of the nine paragraphs. Decide which order they happen in.

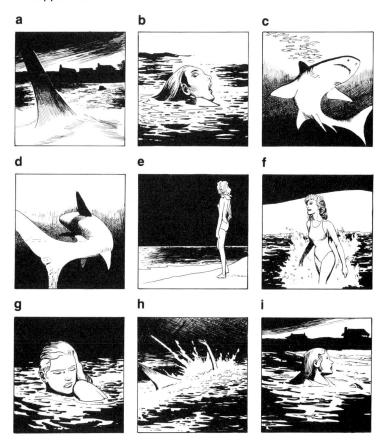

a   b   c

d   e   f

g   h   i

Using paragraphs

Using paragraphs is like using a menu.

Here is an example of a bad menu:

Is it easy to read? How many courses could you have?

1 Imagine you are having a meal at the Halfway Hotel. You want to have three courses, a first course, a main course and a pudding.

Make three lists of what you could have from this confusing menu for each of your three courses.

2 Using your lists copy and complete this easy-to-follow menu.

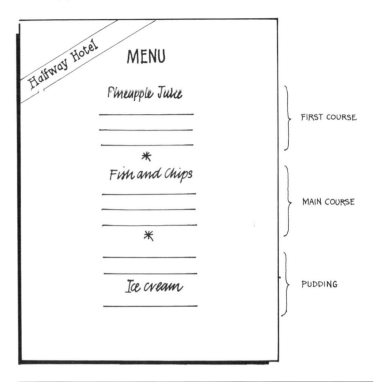

Grouping sentences together into paragraphs is like organising a menu.

3 This chart explains how it works. Read and copy it.

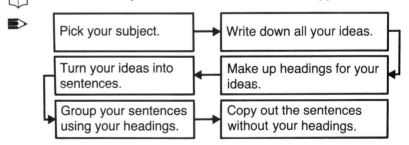

4 Read this page carefully and follow the different stages through. Notice that some words are crossed out when you are doing a draft version like this.

Pick your subject.	~~The music I like~~ A day on the Moon ~~Football~~
Write down all your ideas.	My spacecraft Why I'm there I can ~~bounce up and down~~ float upside down The moon village ~~The~~ moon people The ~~first~~ person I met Moon food ~~What I wearted~~ My moon suit
Make up headings for your ideas.	How I got there What was different What I saw
Turn your ideas into sentences.	I won a competition ~~first prize~~ on earth in the year 2028. The first prize was to go to the moon. On the moon you can float upside down and take huge jumps. My spacecraft was the latest model called a Juno. I saw a moon village made of

lots of plastic bubbles. The moon ~~poeple~~ people ~~wearted~~ wore green suits and spoke into microphones. The first moon person I met was called Jean. Moon food was horrible and looked like slugs. My moon ~~soot~~ suit was silver ~~it~~ and had special zips on the arms and legs.

Group your sentences using your headings.	**How I got there**
	  I won a competition on earth in the year 2028. The first prize was to go to the moon. My space craft was the latest model called a Juno.
	What I saw
	  I saw a moon village made of lots of plastic bubbles. The moon people wore green suits and spoke into microphones. The first person I met was called Jean.
	What was different
	  Moon food was horrible and looked like slugs. My moon suit was silver and had special zips on the arms and legs. On the moon you can float upside down and take huge jumps.

Final draft

<u>21st March 1987</u>

<u>A day on the Moon</u>

I won a competition on Earth in the year 2028. The first prize was to go to the Moon. My space craft was the latest model called a Juno.

I saw a Moon village made of lots of plastic bubbles. The Moon people wore green suits and spoke into microphones. The first Moon person I met was called Jean.

Moon food was horrible and looked like slugs. My Moon suit was silver and had special zips on the arms and legs. On the Moon you can float upside down and take huge jumps.

5 Choose a subject from this list and then write three paragraphs on it. Each subject has some ideas for headings to help you organise your ideas.

   a) *A typical Saturday:* – morning, afternoon, evening out

   b) *The music I like:* – kind of music
                       – information about groups
                       – favourite songs and why

   c) *My best friend:* – name, age and details
                       – why you like her/him
                       – examples of when best friends are helpful

1 In pairs, discuss everything you can see in the picture.

2 What do you think was happening just before the photograph was taken?

3 Imagine you are watching. Write a paragraph on your thoughts as the demonstration goes on.

4 Imagine you are a policewoman on duty. Write a paragraph on *your* thoughts.

The bicycle

In this paragraph about the bicycle, some of the sentences should have been left out as they are not about the bicycle. They have been underlined.

The first kinds of bicycles were called 'hobby-horses'. They had no pedals. The first cars ran on petrol. In 1865 pedals were added to the front wheel. These bicycles were known as 'penny-farthings'. Concorde was a British invention. They had a huge wheel at the front and a small one behind. In 1874 the chain was invented. Hovercrafts can travel over water. Nowadays bicycles have gears and rubber tyres. BMX bicycles are popular for all kinds of racing today.

The ostrich

In this paragraph about the ostrich there are some sentences which do not belong here. Copy out the paragraph, and then underline the ones which do not belong.

When the ostrich is fully grown it is seven or eight feet tall. Elephants live in Africa and India. Its wings haven't developed properly, so it can't fly. Some bicycles can travel at 40 m.p.h. It can travel at 25 m.p.h. Their long feathers are used in fashion design, especially for hats. There are ostrich farms in South Africa. England is in Europe. To help their digestion they eat grit, glass and pebbles.

Answer on page 35

How to ride an ostrich

Riding an ostrich is more difficult than riding a bicycle! Here are four paragraphs which describe one man's attempt to ride an ostrich. Put them in the right order.

A But I was not beaten yet. I tried again and again. When at last I had to give up, my best effort had been two seconds on the back – no more. I staggered back into the house. My legs and arms were bleeding. My bottom was sore. I was covered in dirt. But worst of all, I had been beaten.

B There were a great many visitors who came for a tour of the farm. They began to take an interest in me. I must have been a sight with my torn clothes and many cuts. They would stick their heads through the fence and shout at me. A great cheer went up if I held onto an ostrich for a few yards. But I felt I was at last finding out how to use the wings, not only to stay on but also to steer the bird.

C I crept up from behind. Then I rushed in and snatched a wing. I grabbed the other and jumped at the bird's back. There was only one thing wrong this time. By the time my bottom came down, the bird had already set off. I landed with a jolt in the dust. I was just in time to get a shower of grit in my face.

D Next day I went back to the attack. This time I did not go at it so madly. I tried to get the birds to come close and take the corn from my hand. I set out to get them to trust me.

The blazing car mystery

by *Brian Keaney*

Note: This is a true story.

This is a longer, more difficult piece of writing with its paragraphs in the wrong order. In pairs, decide which order they should be in.

A

Police Constables Bailey and Copping were, naturally enough, asleep when the two men arrived breathless in the village. They woke the police and told them what they had found. All four men rushed back to the scene. The car was still burning but the flames had died down a little. They could make out what looked like a blazing ball in the car. They fetched buckets of water and threw them on the fire. After a while the horrible truth became obvious. What they had taken for a ball was a human head. There was a body in the car!

C

On the way to Cardiff they called in at the Coopers Arms Hotel. Mr Brownhill knew the owner of the hotel and he was chatting to him. He told him about his passenger and how he had had the bad luck to have his car stolen. Just as they were discussing this the butcher's boy came into the room. He had been reading the paper and he said that a body had been discovered in the burnt-out shell of a car. When the butcher's boy said this Mr Rouse seemed to have difficulty controlling himself. He walked out of the room. He was only gone a few minutes and when he returned he was quite himself again. Brownhill took Rouse the rest of the way to Cardiff.

B

Hendall James Brownhill was a car salesman who lived in Cardiff. At about ten o'clock on the morning of the seventh of November he gave a lift to a man called Alfred Rouse who wanted to go to Cardiff. Mr Brownhill agreed and Brownhill and Rouse set off. Mr Rouse was wearing a light mac, a felt hat and he was carrying a small case. He was a talkative type and on the way there he told Brownhill that he had his car stolen the night before last. He said that he had stopped at a restaurant and when he had left the car was gone. He added that later it had been found, burnt. He said that he had reported it to the police and to the insurance company. Mr Brownhill assured him that if he had reported it he had nothing to worry about.

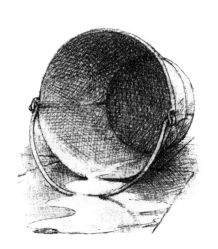

Answer on page 35.

D

When Rouse got off the coach in which he had travelled from Cardiff to London, there were two plain-clothes policemen waiting for him. They asked him to go with them to Hammersmith police-station. He admitted that the car was his. He said he had picked up a hitch-hiker. After driving for some hours he had run out of petrol. He had to go out to go to the toilet and he had asked the hitch-hiker to put some petrol in the tank from the spare can. The hitch-hiker had said 'What about a smoke?' but Rouse had replied 'I have given you all my cigarettes as it is'. The hitch-hiker must have lit up anyway because when Rouse came back the car was in flames. That was his story.

HARDINGSTONE

E

In the early hours of the morning on November 6th, 1930, two men were walking home from a Bonfire Night dance. When they turned off the main road onto Hardingstone Road, which led to the village of Hardingstone where they both lived, they noticed two things: a man climbing out of a ditch opposite and a bright glow ahead of them. They didn't take much notice of the man climbing out of the ditch though they remembered later that he was carrying a small case. Instead they hurried on to see what was causing the blaze. As they got nearer they saw that it was a burning car. The flames were more than fifteen feet high.

When you have decided on the story use it to help you copy these sentences and fill in the missing words.

1 Mr Brownhill was a _____ _____.
2 Mr Rouse was wearing a _____ _____ and a _____ _____.
3 Mr Rouse was carrying a _____ _____.
4 Mr Brownhill and Mr Rouse called in at the _____ _____ Hotel.
5 When Mr Rouse got off the coach there were two _____-_____ _____ waiting for him.

The haunted house

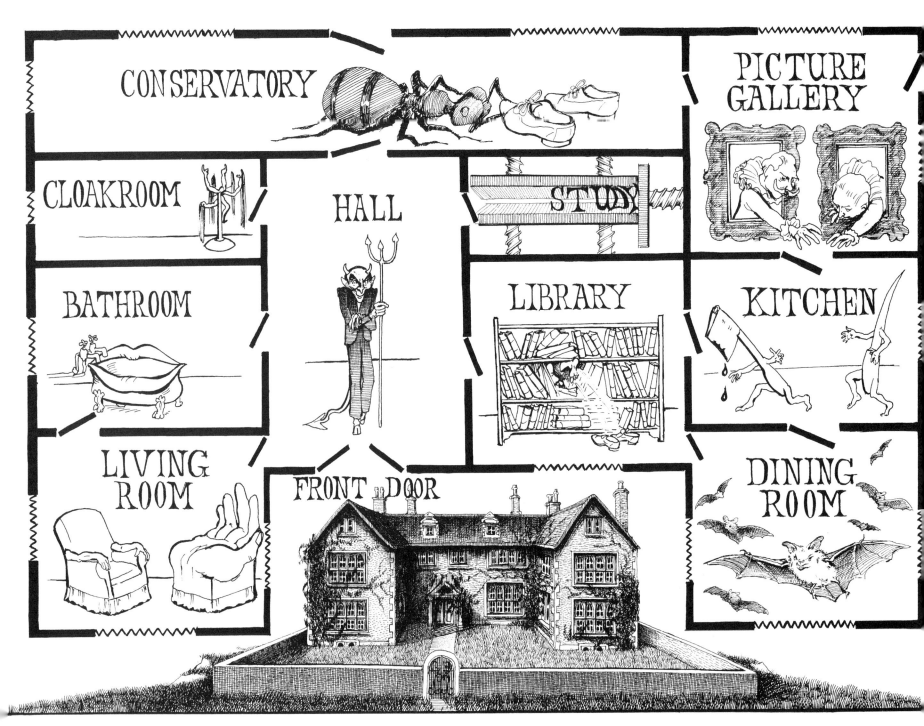

CONSERVATORY

PICTURE GALLERY

CLOAKROOM

STUDY

HALL

BATHROOM

LIBRARY

KITCHEN

LIVING ROOM

FRONT DOOR

DINING ROOM

1 Study the picture and map of this rather unusual house.

2 Imagine you are visiting the house late one night to visit a friend who is staying there. You open the door and are met by a strange creature called the Spook.
You are taken into six different rooms. Choose which six you would like to visit. Make a list of your six and fill it in using these headings.

Room	Unusual feature	How you felt
Dining room	The dining-room was full of vampire bats	I hated the feel of these rat-like creatures which flew past my face as I walked through.

3 When you leave the last of your six rooms the Spook takes you into another room. Decide where. On the floor your friend is lying in a pool of blood. In pairs, decide how she/he was killed.

4 Write a paragraph describing the scene you have just imagined. Say where the body was and what the room was like.

5 You run out of the house and call the police to tell them of the murder. The police ask you for details of what you saw. Write this out in six paragraphs, one for each room. Use your list to help you.
Example:

> The Spook took me into the dining-room. This was next to the kitchen through the library. The dining-room was full of bats. I hated the feel of these rat-like creatures which flew past my face as I walked through.

6 Draw a map for the upstairs floor of the house. Write in your own ideas for unusual goings on in each room. You could add extra ideas for the downstairs rooms, or for outside as well.

Vicar stole car to save a life

Terror strikes haunted house

Schoolboy's charity bid ends in disaster

Teenage girls in hostage drama

Sub-postmaster's bravery award

Death-threat to actor after all-night party

Answers

A How to ride an ostrich (page 31) = C, A, D, B.

B Blazing car mystery (page 32) = E, A, B, C, D.

Personal questionnaire

1 What are you good at? List three things.

....

2 How many good friends do you have?

Who are they? ....

....

3 Do you have a best friend? Yes ☐ No ☐

4 Are you confident? Yes ☐ No ☐ Give an example to back

up your answer ....

5 Do you lose your temper?

often ☐ sometimes ☐ never ☐ Give a typical situation

....

6 Are you a patient person? Yes ☐ No ☐

7 What colour are: your eyes ....

your hair ....

your skin? ....

8 How tall are you? ....

9 Are you thin ☐ slim ☐ small ☐ large ☐

(You make up other words if you don't like these.)

10 What is your favourite:

sport ....

colour ....

food ....

animal ....

music? ....

11 Who do you like best in your family?

....

12 What annoys you most? ....

Explain. ....

13 What makes you laugh? ....

Give an example. ....

14 Who do you dislike most? ....

Explain. ....

15 What is most striking about the way you look? Be honest!

....

16 What makes you afraid? ....

....

17 What makes you special? ....

What do people remember you for?

....

1 Write out your answers to this questionnaire. Try to be completely honest.

2 Choose the five answers which you think are most important, the ones that say most about you. Why have you chosen these five things?

3 Write a paragraph about yourself based on these details. Start off with your name.
Example:

My name is _____
_____

Describing people means saying what they **look** like from the outside and what they **are** like inside.

4 In pairs, describe your partner. Use what you know about her/him already and what you can see with your eyes. Ask questions if you want to find out more.

5 Copy this chart and write your description under these headings:

What s/he looks like	Her/his likes and dislikes	Special features

6 Write a paragraph about your partner using this information.

Bogart

Bogart is a character in a book called *Miguel Street* by V. S. Naipaul. Here are a number of different ways of describing him:

He was the most bored man I ever knew.
He was a man of mystery.
He never told a story.
He lived in a little room.
He was smart.
He never laughed.
He looked like a famous film actor.
He spoke with an American accent.
He would appear and disappear without warning.
He combed his hair backwards.

1 Which of these sentences tell you most about Bogart?

2 Using the sentences you think are most effective, write a longer description of Bogart.

37

Character descriptions

There are many different ways of describing people. The best descriptions bring their characters alive.

Read these descriptions of different people.
After you have read each one, use this chart to ask yourself questions about them.

Title . . . .
1. Does it come alive?
2. What does the person look like?
3. What do you remember about this person?
   Give details.

Two-Bit Mathews

Two-Bit Mathews was the oldest of the gang and the wisecracker of the bunch. He was about six feet tall, stocky in build, and very proud of his long rusty-coloured sideburns. He had grey eyes and a wide grin, and he couldn't stop making funny remarks to save his life. You couldn't shut up that guy; he always had to get his two-bits worth in. Hence his name. Even his teachers forgot his real name was Keith, and we hardly remembered he had one. Life was one big joke to Two-Bit.

by S. E. Hinton

Smiler

It took quite a lot to make Smiler scared. Smiler could look after himself. He was tallish and well-built with a friendly, squarish face, a pressed-in smudge of a nose, and a pair of angelic eyes that, when he put on his special smile, made him look as though butter wouldn't melt in his mouth.

by Victor Canning

Carlie

The girl was Carlie. She was as hard to crack as a coconut. She never said anything polite. When anyone asked how she was, she answered 'What's it to you?' or 'Get lost'. Her main fun was watching television, and she threw things at people who blocked her view. Even the dog had been hit when he stepped in front of the set when Sonny and Cher were singing 'I Got You Babe'.

by Betsy Byars

Samantha

I met Samantha that very first evening and have yet to meet a more beautiful woman. Never had I imagined that there could be a perfect woman. Yet there she was, sitting across from me at supper. Her light-brown hair was fixed in gracefully looping curls down the back of her long white dress. Her eyes were blue, like the sky at dawn. Her voice was soft and low-pitched and made all the more musical by her refined Southern accent, which softened all the harsh sounds I hate in the English language. But as I gazed at her across the table, I always returned to those eyes, for it was there that Samantha lived. Her eyes were the tongue of her soul.

by Julius Lester

Mrs Battle

Mrs Battle came four days a week, Tuesday to Friday, arriving at ten in the morning in a bright red new Volkswagen and leaving at six. She cooked lunch for the children, eating with them in the kitchen while Grandpa and Liz had sandwiches and milk in the study, and laid a cold supper for them all in the dining room. She was a tall, heavy woman with a fuzz of red hair in tight curls and large, gleaming eyes that were the pale grey of fish scales. She showed a lot of pink gum when she laughed, which was often, though not always when something was funny.

by Nina Bawden

The boy

Why, I know lots of things about him, Jane thought suddenly. The boy was at least sixteen, because he had a driver's licence. He had a nice smile and merry eyes – greenish-grey eyes. He had brown hair with a dip in it. He was not really tall, but he was tall enough so a medium-sized girl could wear heels and not feel she had to scrooch down when she walked beside him. He was outdoors a lot, because he was so tanned, and he must be new in Woodmont, because she had never seen him before. He looked like a nice boy, full of fun and – best of all – when he saw she was having trouble with Sandra he understood. One might say they spoke the same language!

by Beverley Cleary

Miss Brown

Miss Brown was a dark, fat lady of medium height. She used the strap more often than any other teacher in the school. Somehow she never asked me any hard questions. I noticed that whenever she asked a question and someone sat there looking lost, she would use her strap to help them remember. If she asked a question, and four or five other persons held their hands up, I would also hold mine up. Because if I got the question wrong, she would think that I was trying and wasn't just a seat warmer. Sometimes I hadn't the faintest idea of what she was asking about, but took a chance and it always paid off.

by Errol O'Connor

Describing places

Describing places is like describing people. It means explaining what they look like and sometimes what it feels like to be there.

The field

The field itself was a long way from home. It was downhill all the way. The field was in a wide, open space. For miles it was green, with trees that rocked from left to right in the midday breeze. There were plants of different types, such as potatoes, tomatoes, and the green long leaves of tobacco. A river divided the wide field into two halves. Footpaths could be seen all around; sometimes they divided a field into sections. Trees of fruits, mangoes, breadfruits and grapes were on the gently sloping hills. Tall, fresh green grass surrounded them, but the cows that ploughed the fields would trample over it as they ate in the evenings.

by Errol O'Connor

25 Cawdour Road

Cawdour Road curved gently to the right and number twenty-five was three-quarters of the way around the curve. The nearest street light was some way away, but it was still easy to make out that, like all the other houses in the road, number twenty-five was detached and had a reasonably sized front garden. The front door had a glass panel in the top and light shone through this. To the right of the front door were bow windows and in the centre of these a thin, jagged line of light showed where the curtains had not quite been drawn together.

by Roderic Jeffries

The pit

After breakfast Barney slipped out of the house and went off to the pit. In the copse the frozen leaves crunched like cornflakes under his feet. He climbed down into the pit on the far side, where the cliff was lowest, and it hurt his fingers to hold onto the icy tree roots. The nettles were all dead in the bottom of the pit and the old cans had lumps of solid ice in them.

by Clive King

 Decide which of these sentences are true and which are false:
a) Cawdour Road was straight.
b) Number 25 was detached.
c) Number 25 had a small garden.
d) The front door had a glass panel in the top.
e) To the right of the front door were bow windows.

 1 One of these descriptions is set in England, and the other one is somewhere in the West Indies. Which words tell you this? Make a list.
2 What do you remember most about each place?

 Look at these pictures and write a description of one of them. Try to bring it alive.

Write a description about a place that you know well. Choose one from the list, or make up one of your own.

Your room
Your home
Your road
Your class
Your school.

It may help to draw it first.

Things to do with descriptions

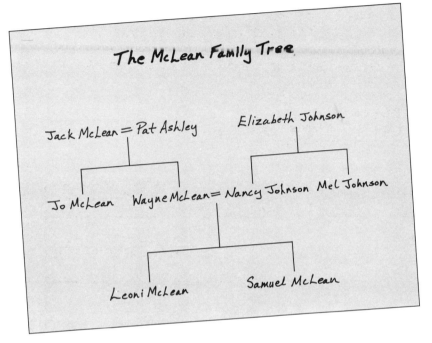

The McLean Family Tree

Jack McLean = Pat Ashley   Elizabeth Johnson

Jo McLean   Wayne McLean = Nancy Johnson   Mel Johnson

Leoni McLean   Samuel McLean

Look at this family tree.
Draw a family tree like this one for your own family.
Choose one person from your family.
Make a list of all you know about that person.
Turn back to page 36 if you need help.
Example:

Mel Johnson
My mum always made me laugh. But then she had had such a tough life herself that she could never really take anything seriously again. She would...

WANTED

Design a **Wanted!** poster for someone famous.
Imagine there is a message on the radio giving a full description.
Example:

```
... Police are looking for a tall man with
dark hair and brown eyes.  He speaks with
an Irish accent and is in the music
business ...
```

Make up a message like this for *your* famous person.

Making up people by numbers

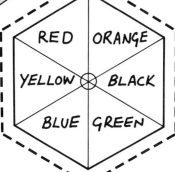

Stage 1
Cut this out and stick it onto some card. Put a pencil through the middle so you can spin it.

Stage 2
Cut out the chart and fill in the spaces with words that could describe people.

Stage 3
Using the chart spin the wheel for each of the six features.
Example: You are deciding on the age of your person. It lands on yellow so she or he will be 15 years old.

Stage 4
Make up a name for your person. Write six sentences to describe her/him.
Example: Rachel is fifteen.

Stage 5
Use your character's name as a heading and write a paragraph made up of six sentences.

FEATURES	Red	Yellow	Blue	Green	Black	Orange
Age	twelve	fifteen			forty	seventy-two
Size						
Special features						
Clothes	grubby		smart	bright	unusual	trendy
Likes						
Where	Swindon	London	Kingston	Karachi	Dublin	

43

What's in a name?

You can have fun with people's names.

Example: My friend Bill
                    Lives half-way up a hill.

Bill sounds like hill.

Stage 1

Make a list of words that sound like these names. Some have been done for you.

1 Fred		dead
2 Bert	dirt	
3 Jane	brain	train
4 John		gone
5 Dave		
6 Jack		
7 Sid	lid	
8 Jim	him	
9 Pete		
10 Jill		

Stage 2

Read this poem about a dog, by Mike Rosen.

Down behind the dustbin
I met a dog called Sid.
He could smell a bone inside
but couldn't lift the lid.

Down behind the dustbin
I met a dog called Sid.
He said he didn't know me,
but I'm pretty sure he did.

Down behind the dustbin
I met a dog called Jim.
He didn't know me
and I didn't know him.

Stage 3

Make up your own poems using the name chart opposite to help you. Copy and complete this:

Down behind the dustbin
I met a dog called ☐.
That's a funny place
_____ ☐.

Note: The last words of the second and last lines must sound the same.

44

Recording your progress in English:

Record sheet 1
(Before you fill this in make sure you have read page 5.)

Name:

Date of recording:

What to do:

:) Tick under this face if you feel confident you can do this well.

:| Tick under this face if you feel you can do this reasonably well.

:(Tick under this face if you feel you need more help in this area.

If you're not sure, leave it blank and fill it in later.

I can:	:)	:|	:(	My comments
write neatly				
write a simple sentence				
use a full stop				
read silently				
listen to a story				
use a tape-recorder				
talk confidently				
recognise a paragraph				
write a paragraph				
give a description				
write a description				
work in a pair				
talk about personal experiences				

45

1. Start with a description of where it happens

2. Write the name of the person speaking in the margin

3. Write what is said next to the name of the character speaking

4. When something happens, write it out like this

5. When a character does something or feels something write it in brackets like this

Joey's return

(The living room of Number 3, St. Catherine's Buildings. The table is set for a feast.)

Rocky: Where's he got to, ma? I ran all the way from school.

Mrs Flanagan: Probably missed his bus, that's all. He'll be here in a minute, don't you fret.

Rocky: I saw Jim Simpson on me way home, drivin' past in his Jag. Keeps trying to talk to me.

Mrs Flanagan: You keep away from that Simpson.

Rocky: He'll keep away from me when our Joey gets out. You won't see him for smoke. Can I have a biscuit, ma?

Mrs Flanagan: You can wait your turn. Anybody'd think I didn't feed yer. This party's for Joey and the first person to touch a mouthful will be him. It's only right and proper.

    *(The door opens and **Joey** stands there.)*

Mrs Flanagan: Talk of the devil and he's sure to appear.

Joey: That's nice, ma, I must say.

    *(**Mrs Flanagan** runs and throws her arms about **Joey**.)*

Mrs Flanagan: Oh, Joey, my boy. It's good to see you home.

    (She starts to weep.)

Joey: *(pushing her away)* OK, ma, I had a bath before I left the nick.

    *(**Mrs Flanagan** takes out a handkerchief and sniffles into it.)*

from *A Pair of Jesus Boots* by Sylvia Sherry

1 What have you found out about Rocky, Mrs Flanagan and Joey from the script?

2 Here's what Joey and Rocky say next but in the wrong order. Decide on the right order and then copy it out. Set it out like the speech on the opposite page. (Joey speaks first.)

a) JOEY : Not bad mate. Could be worse.

b) JOEY : Hello. You've put on an inch or two since I last seen yer.

c) JOEY : Oh ···· yeah.

d) ROCKY : How yer feelin', Joey? What's it like in there?

e) ROCKY : Yer going to stay then?

f) ROCKY : Take mor'n that to put you down, wouldn't it Joey?

Answer on page 55.

3 Continue the script for as many lines as you can.

What would they say?

4 Make up a script involving some or all of these people. Start by giving each one a name. Decide what kind of person each one is. Decide where they could meet. Decide what happens. Write it out as a script.

Doctor Who

The Doctor *and his companions are in the Tardis.*
    (**Peri** *and* **The Doctor** *are studying the console.*)
Peri: (*anxiously*) Well?
The Doctor: I've never felt better.
Peri: Wisecracks like that tell me one thing.
The Doctor: What?
    (*He is absorbed in the controls.*)
Peri: You haven't a clue what's going on.
The Doctor: Oh, I know what's going on. We're being
    manœuvred off course.
Peri: Manœuvred off course! You mean it isn't the
    Tardis malfunctioning again?
The Doctor: Malfunctioning? Malfunctioning? (*shouts*)
    Malfunctioning! After all the work I've done on it!
Peri: I only asked a simple question.
The Doctor: So you did. But it was the wrong question.
    You know how sensitive I am about the Tardis.
Peri: So tell me what's going on.
    (**The Doctor** *peers at the panel.*)
The Doctor: The date co-ordinates are still constant. It's
    just the location that's being changed.
Peri: Being changed! Who by?
The Doctor: I haven't a clue.
    (*Angrily he jabs at the controls.*)
Peri: Can't you override?
The Doctor: Try not to be so obtuse! What d'you imagine
    I'm attempting to do? (*Thinking to himself.*) No. It's
    time distortion. (*Sudden thought*) As though there
    was another time machine nearby.
Peri: A Time Lord?

The Doctor: Or a Dalek. Certainly an alien force of some sort.

Peri: On Earth?

      (**The Doctor** *nods.*)

I don't believe it. Not again. You would think they could find another planet to invade.

by Pip and Jane Baker

1 Read this script taken from *Doctor Who* and compare it with the pictures on both these pages.

2 Draw a plan for a set in this series. Draw a plan of the console with anything else you would expect to find in the Tardis.

3 Draw a picture of the outside of the Tardis or of any other space machine you can imagine.

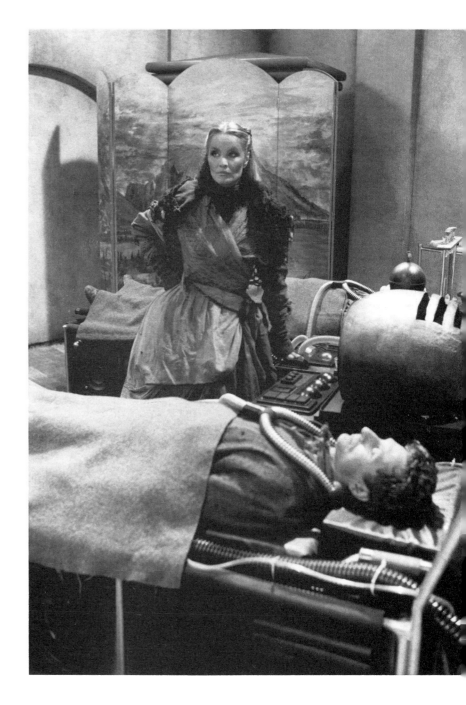

The precinct
by *Brian Keaney*

Scene 1

Malcolm *is standing in the precinct, doing nothing.*
Rodney *comes in.*

Malcolm: Hey Rodney! How ya doing?
Rodney: Bad man, bad. No money, no work, no fun, no future.
Malcolm: Come on. It's not that bad.
Rodney: You know something to cheer me up?
Malcolm: Maybe. Listen, I've got an idea.
Rodney: I'm listening.
Malcolm: You got no money, right?
Rodney: Right.
Malcolm: I got no money either, right?
Rodney: Is this all you got to tell me?
Malcolm: Wait man, wait. Listen. Them people out there buying this, buying that. They got plenty of money.

Rodney: So this is news?
Malcolm: Patience! Listen, they're so anxious to get rid of their money. Maybe we can help them.
Rodney: What are you talking about?
Malcolm: Come on, Rodney. You know what I mean. Let's grab ourselves a little something.
Rodney: Go away Malcolm.
Malcolm: Rodney, are you telling me you're scared?
Rodney: I ain't scared of nothing.
Malcolm: What then?
Rodney: It ain't right.
Malcolm: Is it right that they have money and you and me have nothing?
Rodney: No.
Malcolm: Is it?
Rodney: I just told you, no.
Malcolm: Well then.
Rodney: Well then what?

Malcolm: Well then let's do something to even things out. What's the matter with you?

Rodney: I ain't no thief.

Malcolm: It's not thieving, Rodney.

Rodney: What is it then?

Malcolm: Helping ourselves. Is anyone else going to help us?

Rodney: I don't know.

Malcolm: No one. You know that.

Rodney: I don't care. It's thieving to me. I ain't getting mixed up in it.

Malcolm: Your decision, Rodney. Don't come trying to borrow money off me, that's all.

Rodney: Me borrow money off you, Malcolm. That's a good one. Listen I'm going to the record shop.

Malcolm: What for? You ain't got no money.

Rodney: No, but I got ears ain't I?

Malcolm: OK Rodney, see you later.

Rodney: Yeah man. And hey.

Malcolm: What?

Rodney: Forget about the thieving. OK?

    (**Rodney** *goes off.*)

Scene 2

Maureen *and* **Susan** *are walking along talking.*
Maureen *has a carrier bag in one hand and her purse in the other.*

Maureen: Honestly Susan, you don't know how lucky you are.

Susan: Lucky! You must be joking.

Maureen: No, you are. It's terrible working there now that new supervisor is there. She thinks everybody has to jump whenever she clicks her fingers.

Susan: I don't care. I'd rather be working for her than signing on.

Maureen: I wish somebody would make me redundant.

Susan: You're just saying that.

Maureen: I'm not. I really am fed up with work.

Susan: Well why don't you pack it in then? I could have your job.

Maureen: Cos I need the money of course.

Susan: Don't we all.

Maureen: Do you know how much this sweatshirt cost?

Susan: Look don't Maureen. You'll only make me annoyed.

Maureen: Fifteen pounds! Fifteen pounds. I said to the assistant, 'I don't want a track suit you know. Just a top.'

Susan: Fifteen pounds. You must be mad. They're only six pounds in Hugo's.

Maureen: Not the same quality though, Susan. I mean they're so much thinner.

Susan: Look let's talk about something else, shall we?

Maureen: All right, if you like. You're dead moody nowadays.

Susan: So would you be.

    (*Just then* **Malcolm** *bumps into* **Maureen**.)

Malcolm: Sorry.

Maureen: All right.

    (**Malcolm** *walks off. He has taken* **Maureen's** *purse, but she has not realised.*)

Maureen: Come on Susan. I'll tell you what. I'll buy a cup of coffee. How's that?

Susan: If you like.

Maureen: Well you don't have to have one, you know.

Susan: Sorry. Yes please.

Maureen: Come on then.

Scene 3

Maureen and **Susan** are standing in the queue at the café.

Maureen: Two coffees, please. Do you want a doughnut, Susan?
Susan: I'd better not.
Maureen: Go on. I'm having one.
Susan: Are you sure?
Maureen: Course.
Susan: All right.
Maureen: Two doughnuts, please.
Woman: One-forty-eight please.
Maureen: My purse! Where's my purse? Susan have you got it?
Susan: No. You haven't lost it, have you?
Maureen: Oh no! I think I must have. I'm sorry, I can't pay for this.
Woman: What am I supposed to do now? I've rung it up as well.
Maureen: I'm sorry.
    (**Maureen** and **Susan** walk out of the café.)
Maureen: I know! I bet it was that bloke!
Susan: What bloke?
Maureen: The one who bumped into me. Remember? I'm sure I had it in my hand before that.
Susan: Must have been. Come on. Let's find a policeman.

Scene 4

Rodney is standing in the record shop looking at LPs. **Malcolm** comes in.

Malcolm: OK Rodney?
Rodney: Hey Malcolm listen to this.
Malcolm: To what?

Rodney: This record, man. I love it. They play it over and over again in this shop. They've got good taste here.
Malcolm: Yeah it's OK.
Rodney: OK! Man it's brilliant.
    (**Rodney** closes his eyes and moves in time with the music. He is carried away. **Maureen** and **Susan** come into the record shop with a **Policeman**. **Malcolm** sees them and pushes the purse into **Rodney's** pocket.)
Maureen: Just a minute. I think it was him.
Policeman: Quietly, please. Who?
Maureen: One of those two over there.
Policeman: Which one?
Maureen: I don't know. I only saw him for a second.
Susan: I think it was the one with his eyes closed.
Policeman: OK. Look could one of you go outside and ask a couple of the security men to stand outside the door in case someone tries to make a run for it. You'll find two of them just beside the children's play area.
Susan: I'll go.
    (**Susan** goes out.)

Policeman: Now please try to remember. Which one was it?

Maureen: Honestly I just can't.

Policeman: Well never mind. I'll just have to search both of them.

Maureen: I don't know for certain that they took it.

Policeman: Well if they're innocent they won't have anything to hide, will they?

(**Susan** *comes back into the shop*.)

Susan: They're outside.

Policeman: Right.

(**Policeman** *walks over to* **Malcolm** *and* **Rodney**.)

Policeman: Excuse me but a complaint has been made by this woman that her purse has been stolen. She believes that one of you two may be responsible. Would you mind showing me what's in your pockets.

Rodney: What is this? I ain't no thief. I don't know what you're talking about.

Policeman: I'm simply asking you to show me what's in your pockets. Unless you'd rather show me down at the station.

Rodney: This is harassment. I ain't doing nothing wrong. I'm just listening to music. I suppose there's a law against that now.

(**Malcolm** *takes various things out of his pockets: coins, a letter, a box of matches*.)

Malcolm: Look. This is all I've got in my pockets. OK?

(*The* **Policeman** *makes a quick check by patting* **Malcolm** *up and down. He takes the letter*.)

Policeman: Malcolm Tillyard, 16 Brookbank Road. Is that you?

Malcolm: Yes.

(**Policeman** *takes out a notebook and pen and writes the address down*.)

Malcolm: Can I go now?

Policeman: Yes. We may be in touch later.

(*The* **Policeman** *turns back to* **Rodney**. **Malcolm** *leaves*.)

Policeman: Now if you would just co-operate like your friend.

Rodney: I don't see why I should have to put up with this abuse.

Policeman: Nobody's abusing you. Now I'm asking you for the last time to turn out your pockets.

Rodney: OK, OK. Look I've got a dirty handkerchief in this pocket, right? And in this one...

(**Rodney** *stops suddenly. He has discovered the purse.*)

Policeman: Can you show me what you have in your hand, please?

Rodney: It's a plant. I don't know nothing about it. I've never seen it before.

Policeman: I'll take that. Thank you. Is this the purse, madam?

Maureen: Yes, that's it.

Policeman: Now then. I'm arresting you for the theft of this purse and I'd like you to come down to the police station with me where you will be charged.

Rodney: It's a fix. Wait a minute! I see it. It was him, Malcolm! That snake in the grass.

Policeman: Come on then.

Rodney: You don't understand. It was him. The one you just let walk out of here. He took the purse. I know he did.

Policeman: You can tell me all about it down at the station. Come on.

(*The* **Policeman** *leaves with* **Rodney**.)

➡️ Write out as a script, *either*

a) what Rodney said to the policeman at the police station
or
b) what Rodney said to Malcolm next time he saw him.

Telephone lines

1 Compare this picture with the details next to it.

Ms X

Name ...... Mary Tollitt ......
Age ...... 34 ....
Address .49, Oak Lane
.... Liverpool ....
Tel no ..723567............
Occupation (1) Chemist (part time)
...... (2) Bringing up children!

Mrs C

Mrs D

2 For each of these people make up a name, their age, an address in Liverpool, telephone number and an occupation. Set it out like the example above.

Ms A

Mr B

Mr E

All these people are on the telephone in Liverpool where they live.
Example:

Tollitt, M 49 Oak Lane, Liverpool 723576

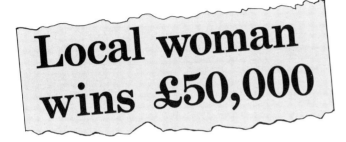

Ms A has won £50,000. Her postman Mr E knows because he heard her scream of excitement when he delivered the post. He rings the local TV station. Ms X rings Ms A to ask her what she is going to do with the money and if she will do a TV interview.

3 Use this suggestion for an unusual telephone call and, in pairs, make one up. Use the names and any other details you have decided on. Decide how the money was won.
Example:

Miss ..... Liverpool 572346, Beverley here.
Ms ..... Hello is that Miss .... speaking?
Miss .... Yes, who's speaking?
Ms ..... It's ..... from the BBC. I
gather you have just won
£50,000 on ......

Local man in mystery accident

4 Make up a situation involving Mrs C, Ms X, Mr B and Mr E. There is some kind of accident and Mr B and Mrs C are taken to hospital. Ms X saw what happened as she was walking to work.

Decide on your situation and then make up a telephone call between
a) Mrs C and her sister (to say what happened).
b) Ms X and the hospital (to see how they are).
Try and make the calls as realistic as possible with plenty of details.

Liverpool stages earthqake concert

5 There has been a huge concert in Liverpool to raise money for the victims of an earthquake.
a) Decide how *all* the people on the opposite page could have been involved in this event.
Examples: Mr B is reporting it for BBC TV.
Mr E has bought tickets to hear his favourite singer Ms A, etc.
b) Make up a telephone conversation between two of these people *or* a scene involving some of them. Try to use several different people. Write it out as a script.

Answer

Rocky and Joey (page 47) = B, D, A, F, C, E.

55

Setting out a letter

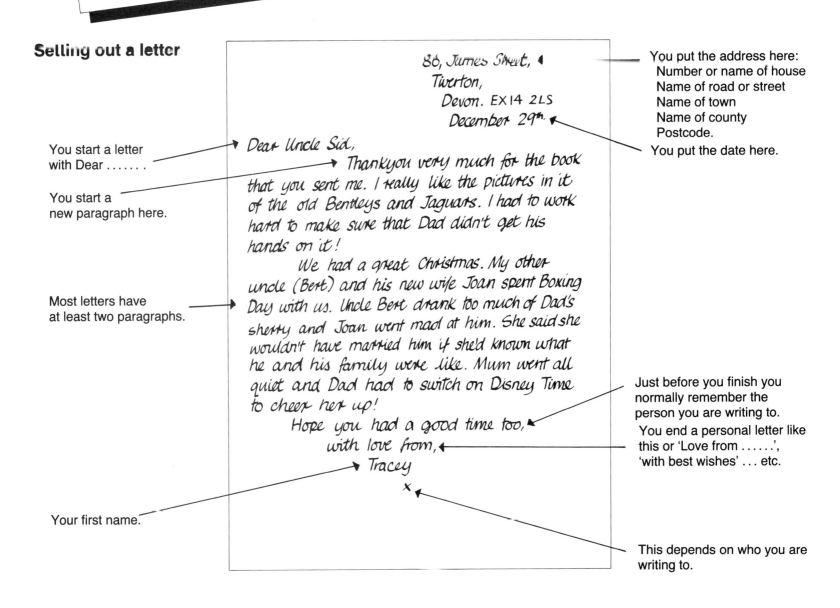

You put the address here:
- Number or name of house
- Name of road or street
- Name of town
- Name of county
- Postcode.

You put the date here.

You start a letter with Dear ....

You start a new paragraph here.

Most letters have at least two paragraphs.

Just before you finish you normally remember the person you are writing to.

You end a personal letter like this or 'Love from ......', 'with best wishes' ... etc.

Your first name.

This depends on who you are writing to.

The letter reads:

86, James Street,
Tiverton,
Devon. EX14 2LS
December 29th.

Dear Uncle Sid,

Thankyou very much for the book that you sent me. I really like the pictures in it of the old Bentleys and Jaguars. I had to work hard to make sure that Dad didn't get his hands on it!

We had a great Christmas. My other uncle (Bert) and his new wife Joan spent Boxing Day with us. Uncle Bert drank too much of Dad's sherry and Joan went mad at him. She said she wouldn't have married him if she'd known what he and his family were like. Mum went all quiet and Dad had to switch on Disney Time to cheer her up!

Hope you had a good time too,
with love from,
Tracey
x

1 Choose one of these situations, and write a personal letter about it.

a) You have been sent a birthday present by someone in your family. You don't like the present! Decide what it is. Write a thank-you letter for it and describe what you did on your birthday.

b) Your school has been paired with a school in Jamaica. Everyone in your class is going to have a pen friend of their own age. You are given this picture and brief description. Write back with information about yourself.

Name Rachel Selvon
I live in Kingston with my family.
I have two brothers and two
sisters. My father works for the
Post Office. I like reggae music and
also electro-funk. I am hoping to be
in the school cricket team next year.

c) You are interested in a particular pop group. You want to find out more about them and possibly join a fan club. Decide which group. Write to them telling them why you like them and what you would like to do.

Setting out the address

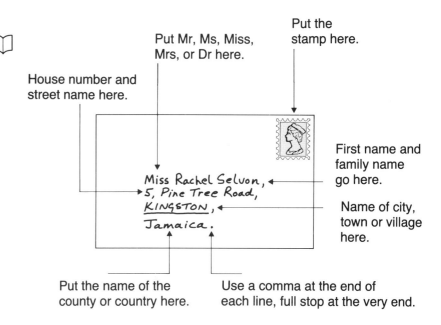

Put Mr, Ms, Miss, Mrs, or Dr here.

Put the stamp here.

House number and street name here.

Miss Rachel Selvon,
5, Pine Tree Road,
KINGSTON,
Jamaica.

First name and family name go here.

Name of city, town or village here.

Put the name of the county or country here.

Use a comma at the end of each line, full stop at the very end.

Sending a postcard

Draw the outline of a postcard the right size. Imagine you are on holiday. Decide where you are. Fill in the left-hand side with what you would write to one of your friends. Write the address of your friend on the right-hand side, setting it out as shown above.

ADDRESS

Dear Zelda, 1

I'm having terrible arguments with my girlfriend at the moment and I thought you might be able to help. I like to stay at home and watch television or listen to records, because I like to be with her on her own. She gets annoyed and starts arguing with me.

I can't give you my name because she would make fun of me for writing to you. Can you help?

A reader in Yorkshire.

Dear Zelda, 3

I think your problem page is full of stupid people's ideas. Anyone who writes to magazines like yours must be really pathetic. Why on earth do you bother? Nobody reads them.

Stephen, London.

Dear Zelda, 5

I'm 15 and going out with an Indian boy. My parents have told me not to see him again. Every time I try to talk to them about it, they don't want to know.

My boyfriend says everything will work out in the end, but I feel very upset. Please don't tell me to finish with my fella because I love him too much and I'm determined that nothing will break us up.

Julie, Edinburgh.

Dear Zelda, 4

I am a fourteen year old girl and I go to a lot of football matches both at home and away. I think the reason that there is so much trouble is that too many boys and not enough girls watch and play football.

My boyfriend thinks it's big to get involved in fights but I tell him he's being stupid. Maybe it would be better if boys had to go to matches with a female member of their family. What do you think?

Alison, Reading.

Dear Zelda, 2

I know this sounds silly but I really want to run away from home. If it wasn't for my mum and dad, and school, I'm sure I would. I live in a small village and there's nothing to do. I see the same old faces every day, and sometimes I cry about the good times I could be having if I lived in the city.

The only disco is miles away and I'm not interested in the village lads. What can I do?

Lorraine, Humberside.

Zelda the Agony Aunt

Here are some letters to Zelda the Agony Aunt. (Notice that they are set out in a much simpler way than the letters you have practised.)

1 Match up each of these pictures with the writer of each letter.

a

b

c

d

e

2 How much more can you say about the people who wrote each of the letters? Can you tell:
  a) their age
  b) the kind of person they are
  c) anything else?

3 Imagine you are Zelda. Decide what advice you would give to each of the letter writers. Choose two and write replies to them in the form of an 'agony letter'.
Example:

Dear Stephen

Thank you for taking the time to write to our problem page. You obviously enjoy reading it.

As you can see there are many real problems expressed in the other letters, problems common to many people.

My only advice to you is to be a little less big-headed and more understanding in future.

Zelda

4 Make up a problem page of your own. (You could look at magazines to give you ideas.)
Write a number of agony letters and choose someone to write replies to each one. When you have finished write them all out together.

Shady customers

by *Brian Keaney*

It was from the children that Mrs Kingston first got the idea. They were always boasting about how good they were at it. They even wrote about it in the essays that she set them from time to time. She had often wondered whether they were telling the truth or not. She had never stolen anything when she was a child but then she had always been quiet. As she walked towards the bookshop on her way back from school she got that excited feeling in her stomach. It was the ideal place. She had bought books there in the past. The shop-assistant had smiled at her the last time she was in there. Even if they noticed she could probably talk her way out of it.

Linda was at the cash desk where she always sat. There weren't quite so many people in the shop as usual. There were one or two regular customers: the vicar of St Marks, the woman with the grey hair whom Linda thought was a teacher in the school down the road. Then there were some people she had never seen before. One of them made her think of what the manager had been saying to her earlier about shop-lifting. He was a bit scruffy-looking and had a way of looking around all the time at the other customers that made Linda suspicious. 'I'll have to keep an eye on that one,' she told herself. She was still thinking about book thieves when she noticed the grey-haired lady standing in front of her. As Linda looked up, the woman came forward and asked about a book she wanted. When Linda told her where it was she walked off, looking very anxious and very old. Linda couldn't help thinking what a strain it must be teaching, especially these days.

Mrs Kingston saw the shop-assistant looking at her and her knees began to buckle. 'Pull yourself together,' she told herself, but she seemed to have lost all control over her body. Why on earth had she gone over and asked about Roald Dahl? She had wanted to show that she was here for a purpose, but all she had done was draw attention to herself. As she was thinking this she realised that someone else was looking at her. A rather scruffy-looking man was wandering about the shop and quite definitely watching her. He was the store-detective! She was certain of it. Her heart began to pound so fast she felt certain it would burst. He must have seen her put the book in her bag! How could she possibly leave now? She would go to the counter, take the book out of her bag and pay for it. That was the only way out. She began to walk towards the counter but she could not bring herself to do it. She turned off again to study a display of books on cookery. She had to go through with this thing. No matter what happened she had to try. If she left now after paying for the book she would only come back another time and try again.

She looked up from the display. To her amazement the shop-assistant had gone. It was now or never! Without looking right or left she marched out of the shop and down the road as fast as she could.

Jim looked up. She was gone. He couldn't believe it. Well perhaps she wasn't the store-detective after all. She was acting very strangely for a customer, though. There was no one at all in the shop now except for himself and the vicar. God knows where the shop-assistant had gone. To spend a penny probably. He was tempted to grab a few more books but then he wasn't sure about the grey-haired woman. Maybe she was a store-detective. She might have gone to get a policeman. Best get out while the going's good, he decided. He put his hands in his pockets and walked quickly out of the shop. Just as the big glass door was closing behind him he felt a hand on his shoulder. He turned to see Linda and the manager. 'Would you mind stepping into the shop for a moment,' the manager was saying. Jim thought about making a break for it but he was rooted to the spot. What was the point, anyway? The grey-haired woman would be back with the police at any moment. She had been watching him all the time. And she looked so harmless, he thought to himself. Crafty old bag.

Dear Zelda,
I am a fifty year old woman. I have worked as a teacher in a Secondary school for the last thirty years. I am a widow and have no close family. I have given most of my energy to my job.

Recently, however, I have begun to have a terrible urge to steal. I have never done anything illegal in my life, but now every time I go into a shop I start imagining what it would be like to take something and walk out of the shop without paying for it.

I am terribly afraid that if I go on like this, sooner or later I shall give in to temptation. What shall I do? Please help me to help myself.

Yours sincerely,
Mrs W. K.

 1 In pairs, talk about what Mrs Kingston did and why you think she did it.

2 What do you think of the last line of the story? Is it fair?

3 Read the start of this agony letter from another character in the story, Jim. Copy and complete it.

Dear Zelda,
I know that most of your readers are women, but I read your magazine at the doctor's the other day and I thought you might be able to help me...

4 Imagine you are Linda from the story. Make up a problem for her and write another agony letter.

Family letters

A day out

1 Imagine you have just had a day out like this. Make a list of the things you did using the pictures to help you. You could add other ideas of your own.

2 Write a letter to your grandparent thanking her/him for the day.

Christmas thank you's

Dear Auntie
Oh, what a nice jumper
I've always adored powder blue
and fancy you thinking of
orange and pink
for the stripes
how clever of you!

Dear Uncle
The soap is
terrific
So
useful
and such a kind thought and
how did you guess that
I'd just used the last of
the soap that last Christmas brought?

Dear Gran
Many thanks for the hankies
Now I really can't wait for the flu
and the daisies embroidered
in red round the 'M'
for Michael
how
thoughtful of you!

Dear Cousin
What socks!
and the same sort you wear
so you must be
the last word in style
and I'm certain you're right that the
luminous green
will make me stand out a mile

Dear Sister
I quite understand your concern
it's a risk sending jam in the post
But I think I've pulled out
all the big bits
of glass
so it won't taste too sharp
spread on toast

Dear Grandad
Don't fret
I'm delighted
So *don't* think your gift will
offend
I'm not at all hurt
that you gave up this year
and just sent me
a fiver
to spend

Mick Gower

Think up the six most useless or stupid presents that you could receive for your birthday. Decide which members of your family gave them to you. Make up thank-you letters to the senders, and write them out like a poem. Head your poem *Birthday Thank You's*.

Sonny's lettah

Read this letter *out loud*. You will have to read it more than once and listen carefully to the sounds of the words.

Dear Mama,
Good Day.
I hope dat wen
deze few lines reach y'u,
they may find y'u in di bes' af helt.

Mama,
I really doan know how fi tell y'u dis,
cause I did mek a salim pramis
fi tek care a lickle Jim
an' try mi bes' fi look out fi him.

Mama,
Ah really did try mi bes',
but none-di-les',
mi sarry fi tell y'u seh
poor lickle Jim get arres'.

It woz di miggle a di rush howah
wen everybady jus' a hus'le an' a bus'le
fi goh home fi dem evenin' showah;
mi an' Jim stan-up
waitin' pan a bus,
nat causin' no fus',
wen all an a sudden
a police van pull-up.

Out jump t'ree policeman,
di 'hole a dem carryin' batan.
Dem waak straight up to mi an' Jim.
One a dem hol' an to Jim
seh him tekin him in;
Jim tell him fi let goh a him
far him noh dhu not'n',
an him naw t'ief,
nat even a but'n.
Jim start to wriggle.
Di police start to giggle.

Mama,
mek Ah tell y'u whey dem dhu to Jim;
Mama,
mek Ah tell y'u whey dem dhu to him:

dem t'ump him in him belly
an' it turn to jelly
dem lick him pan him back
an' him rib get pap
dem lick him pan him he'd
but it tuff like le'd
dem kick him in him seed
an' it started to bleed

Mama,
Ah jus' could'n' stan-up deh
an' noh dhu not'n':
soh mi jook one in him eye
an' him started to cry;
mi t'ump one in him mout'
an' him started to shout
mi kick one pan him shin
an' him started to spin
mi t'ump him pan him chin
an' him drap pan a bin

an' crash
an de'd.

Mama,
more policeman come dung
an' beat mi to di grung;
dem charge Jim fi sus;
dem charge mi fi murdah.

Mama,
doan fret,
doan get depres'
an' doun-hearted
Be af good courage
till I hear fram you.

I remain,
your son,
Sonny.

L. K. Johnson

Note: This poem was written in protest at the 'sus' law which
allowed the police to stop people on *sus*picion only. This
law no longer exists.

In pairs, work out what this letter is about.
Write it out in some of your own words.

Here are some words to help you:
lickle = little   *t'ief* = thief   *t'ump* = thump
sus = suspicion   *murdah* = murder

Unit 7: Making notes

Telephone messages

1 In pairs take it in turns to read these two telephone messages aloud while your partner tries to write the message down.

    a) *When you are reading the message*
    Imagine you are in a call-box with only one 10p piece. Read quickly and clearly. There is no time for you to repeat anything.

    b) *When you are writing down the message*
    Listen carefully and try and get the message down on paper. There is no chance of it being repeated.

> Hello ... it's dad here ... I'm going to be late and couldn't get to the shops ... Grandad's coming to supper and I won't have time to get anything ... Could you buy a tin of tomatoes, some mince, some onions and a packet of spaghetti from the supermarket? There's money in the kitchen drawer ... See you about 7. Bye ...

> Hi ... it's Rupinder here ... could you leave Robert a message ... it's very urgent ... Tell him I've got two tickets – £6.50 each – to see Rosie and the Red Bats next Saturday. If he wants one of them could he ring me tonight? ... My number is 241890 .. Thanks a lot ...

2 Compare what you have written down. If you were left your partner's message, would it make sense?

3 Give your message a title.

> URGENT MESSAGE FROM RUPINDER

4 Copy out one of the messages in full. Underline all the most important or key words.

> Hello ... it's <u>Dad here</u> ... I'm <u>going to be late</u> and <u>couldn't get to the shops</u> ... <u>Grandad's coming to supper</u> and I won't have time ...

Remember: Key words are the most important words. Don't just copy down every word.

5 Use your underlined passage to make a shorter message.

> Dad rang. Going to be late – couldn't get to shops. Grandad's coming to supper...

Write it out with a clear title. Leave plenty of space.

Other messages

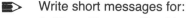

Write short messages for:

1 *The milkman* telling him you are going away on holiday for two weeks and won't be needing any milk. You'll pay him when you return.

2 *A neighbour* telling her you are expecting the gas meter reader to come and would like her to let him in. You've left a key and will be back at about six o'clock.

> Notes are like messages. You use only the key words to keep them short. You make sure they can be clearly understood. You don't need to use complete sentences.

Shortening words

Sometimes you can shorten words to save time.

> Short forms of words are called abbreviations.

1 Match up the short forms with the longer words. Think of other short forms as well.

st.	street	shd.	could
photo	television	wd.	would
eg.	plus	+	photograph
etc.	information	TV	for example
&	should	cd.	etcetera
info.	and		

Lists

1 Make a shopping list of all the things you can see in this picture.

2 Make a numbered list of the important points in this recipe for wholemeal bread. It was written very quickly and you are trying to make it easier to understand.

You will need to put some flour and salt into a large bowl and make a well in the middle of it. Then you must put some yeast into a small bowl with some water. You can leave it to froth. Add some honey to some more water. Melt some fat and let it cool. When you've done all this, pour all the liquids into the well in the flour and mix it all up until it feels like putty. You can leave the bread mixture to rise. When it is twice as big turn it out of the bowl and cut it into four pieces. Then put the dough into baking tins. Sprinkle the dough with flour. Bake in a hot oven for about 40 minutes.

Example:

HOW TO MAKE
WHOLEMEAL BREAD

1. Put flour and salt into a large bowl.
2. Make a well in the middle of the flour.
3. Put yeast in small bowl...

Remember: There are many kinds of useful notes. Use some or all of these ideas to help you.

a) Key words   d) Numbering points
b) Headings   e) Plenty of space
c) Underlinings   f) Abbreviations

67

Planet earth

 1 Imagine you are from another planet. You have been sent to Earth as a scout to explore it to see if it would be a good place for your people to live. Your satellite has taken these six pictures and your task is to prepare brief notes so that you can report back to your leader.

Here are some headings to use in your notes. You may want to make up others:

- Temperature/Climate
- Description of place
- Description of aliens
- Particular problems

2 Using your notes present your opinions to a group. Decide which place you would choose if you were from another planet and why.

Remember: Making notes at home or in school can help you to:

- find out what you think
- organise what you think
- remember more
- remember the important points

Try making notes on a lesson at school and see if it helps your memory.

68

Rules and regulations

The machine-gunners

Chas and his friends have found a real machine-gun and made a hideout for it. They pretend that they are in the army, call their hideout Fortress Caparetto and make up rules for it.

⊙ Chas's heart glowed with pride. All done in a fortnight and as dry as a bone. And a notice-board marked *Fortress Caparetto – Standing Orders*. Chas was not quite sure what Standing Orders were, so they were read out twice a day, with everybody standing up respectfully.

1 Anyone who steals food from the Fortress, if found guilty by Court Martial, shall be thrown in the goldfish pond. They may take off any clothes they want to first, but Keep It Decent.
2 Anyone touching the Gun without permission will be chucked out of the Fortress for Three Months. Anyone who speaks to Boddser Brown for any reason will be chucked out for Good.
3 Anyone lying on the bunks will tidy up afterwards.
4 No peeing within fifty yards, or Anything Else.
5 Always come in by the back fence, after making sure you're not followed.
6 No stealing from shops without permission. All goods stolen belong to the Fortress.
7 Only sentries will touch the air-rifle. Hand back all pellets out of your pockets etc. when coming off duty.
8 Do not mess about with catapults inside the Fortress or you will wash up for four days.
9 Do not mess about at all.
10 Penalty for splitting to parents, teachers etc. is DEATH.

by Robert Westall

Tom Sawyer's gang

Tom is forming a gang and, like Chas, decides that every gang must have its own rules. Some of the words used are explained at the end. These words are underlined.

⊙ **Tom**: Now I'm gonna start a band of robbers. The hideout's in the quarry cave. It'll be called Tom Sawyer's Gang, and everybody that wants to join'll have to take an <u>oath</u> and write his name in blood. Is everyone agreed?
Gang (*variously*): We don't know yet. We ain't heard the oath. Yes. Sure. Let's hear it. What's it say?
Tom (*producing piece of paper from his pocket*): Well, every member of the gang must swear to stick to the band. And if anybody does anything to anyone in the gang, whichever boy is ordered to kill that person and his family must do it and afterwards hack a cross in their breasts, which is the sign of the gang. And nobody that doesn't belong to the gang can use that mark, and if they do they must be <u>sued</u>; and if they do it again, they must be killed. And if any member of the gang tells its secrets, he must have his throat cut and his name blotted off of the list with blood, and never mentioned again by the gang, but have a <u>curse</u> put on it and be forgot for ever.
Johnny: Gee, Tom, that's a real beautiful oath. (*General agreement.*)
Joe: Did you make it up out of your own head?
Tom: Well, some of it. The rest was out of pirate books and robber books. Every gang that amounts to anything has it.
Jeff: *I* reckon we ought to kill the *families* of anyone that tells the secrets as well. (*General agreement.*)
Tom: Well, I'm agreed.
Joe: But Huck ain't got a family we can kill. What you gonna do about him?

Tom: He's got a father, ain't he?

Ben: 'Cept you can't ever find him these days.

Johnny: 'Course you can. He's always laying drunk with the hogs in the tan-yard.

Joe: Used to be, you mean.

Jeff: He ain't been seen around for more'n a year now.

Ben: So he can't come in.

Joe: But it ain't Huck's fault.

Jeff: That don't matter. Every boy has to have a family or somebody to kill, or else it wouldn't be fair and square for the others.

Huck: What about Muff Potter? He gives me food sometimes. You could kill him.

Boys (*variously*): Oh, he'll do, he'll do. That's all right. Huck can come in.

Tom: Yes, Muff'll do for a family.

Dave: So that's settled.

Ben: Now what's the line of business of this gang?

Tom: Nothin' only robbery and murder – suchlike high-toned stuff. We're kinda highwaymen. We stop stages and carriages on the road, with masks on, and kill the people and take their watches and money.

by *John Charlesworth* and *Tony Brown*
(adapted from the novel, *Tom Sawyer*, by Mark Twain)

an oath = a solemn promise
sued = taken to the law courts
a curse = an evil spell
hogs = pigs
highwaymen = robbers

Make a list of the rules for Tom's gang. Write them out like those from *The machine-gunners* on page 70. Include anything that Tom or his gang agree on in the passage you have just read.
Example:

> ## RULES OF TOM SAWYER'S GANG
>
> 1. The gang's hideout's in the quarry cave.
> 2. It'll be called Tom Sawyer's gang.
> 3. Everybody must take an oath and...

Your gang

Imagine you are setting up a gang yourself. Write down ten rules for it.

Games

Using numbered points, write down the rules for any game you know.
Example:

The rules of darts

1 You throw 3 darts at the board.
2 You take it in turns.
3 You have to score exactly 501.
4 The outer ring is called a double.
5 The inner ring is called a treble.
6 You have to start and finish with a double.

Note-making: Things to do

House-hunting

1 You work for a firm of Estate Agents. You have a number of houses for sale and a number of people wanting to buy them.

Types of housing possible

detached house

semi-detached house

terraced house

bungalow

cottage

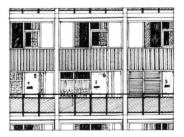

flat

PROPERTY FOR SALE

EASTLEIGH   £70,000

* Village location
* 4 bedrooms
* Superb kitchen
* Central heating
* Garage
* Large garden
* Built in 1960

OXFORD   £55,000

* Central location
* 3 bedrooms
* 2 bathrooms
* Central heating
* Small private garden
* Street parking
* Built in 1930

BRIDLINGTON   £17,000

* House of great character
* 3 bedrooms
* Fine view of the city
* Needs modernisation
* Garage
* Garden
* Built in 1890

PROPERTY FOR SALE

d

PMINSTER £35,000

Set in quiet village
2 bedrooms
Large sitting-room
Small garden
Garage
Built in 1969

e

RAFTON £50,000

In popular village
Thatched roof
2 bedrooms
Small garden
Built in 1810

f

ANSGATE £28,000

Compact flat close to city
2 bedrooms
Central heating
No garden
Parking space available

Possible buyers

Mrs Carter

I am looking for a bungalow or flat with a garden. I need at least 2 bedrooms. I want a modern property with a garage. I can afford up to £45,000. **1**

Mr and Mrs Lawn-Upton

We want a large house with at least 3 bedrooms. It must have central heating and we would like a detached house if possible. We can go up to £75,000. **2**

Mr Bradley

I want a house that's easy to run, small and preferably with no garden. It must have somewhere for my car. I can stretch to £30,000. **3**

Ms Andrews

I want a cottage or an old terraced house. The house must be attractive. I want at least 2 bedrooms and I don't mind about a garden. I could just afford £35,000. **4**

1 Make a list of all the houses that might suit each buyer.

G **2** Decide which houses best suit which people, and write it down.

3 Make up more descriptions of houses and more possible buyers and continue to practise your note-making.

A doctor's surgery

by Brian Keaney

Scene 1

Doctor: Good morning Ms Baker. What can I do for you?

Patient: It's these marks on my arm doctor. See this one here. It's a sort of red circle and it keeps getting bigger. The other one's just the same.

Doctor: Yes, I see. That looks like ringworm. Have you been in contact with any animals?

Patient: Oh no doctor, it's not worms. It's just this red mark, see. And it's sort of greyish in the middle. It's rather itchy. It's just some sort of skin infection. It couldn't be worms.

Doctor: Ringworm is a skin infection, Ms Baker. It's not caused by a worm at all. It's a fungus like athlete's foot.

Patient: Oh no, doctor. It's not on my foot at all, just my arm.

Doctor: Yes well it shouldn't be any problem. I'll write you a prescription for some Whitfield's ointment which I want you to put on twice a day. That should clear it up.

Patient: Thank you doctor. I knew it wasn't worms.

Scene 2

Doctor: Good morning Mr O'Riordan. What seems to be the problem?

Patient: It's this swelling on my wrist.

Doctor: Let me have a look. Oh yes. When did this appear?

Patient: Yesterday.

Doctor: What job do you do?

Patient: I'm a secretary.

Doctor: Do you do a lot of typing?

Patient: Yes, especially recently.

Doctor: Well that may be what's caused it. What you've got is a ganglion cist.

Patient: Is that serious?

Doctor: Oh not really. Excuse me a minute while I get down this medical dictionary.

Patient: But what is it?

Doctor: Oh it's just a build up of fluid around the joint, caused by excessive exercise usually.

Patient: But what can I do about it?

Doctor: Well they sometimes go away of their own accord, or you could go into hospital to have it lanced. In the old days they used to burst them with a bible.

Patient: Burst them with a bible?

Doctor: Yes but it doesn't have to be a bible. A medical dictionary will do. We could try it if you like. Just put your hand on the corner of the desk and I'll hit it with the dictionary. Of course it will probably hurt a little.

Patient: Thank you doctor. I think I'll wait and see if it clears up on its own.

Scene 3

Doctor: Sit down Mrs Cumberbunch. What's the problem?

Patient: I think I'm going deaf, doctor.

Doctor: Oh yes. What makes you think that?

Patient: I beg your pardon.

Doctor: Why do you think that?

Patient: I can't hear what people are saying to me.

Doctor: I'll just have a look in your ears. Oh yes, there's quite a build up of wax there. They will have to be syringed.

Patient: I don't know what I'm going to do; I'm only 30. I'll lose my job if they find out I'm going deaf. I think they know already. I have to keep asking people to repeat what they've just said.

Doctor: There's nothing to worry about.

Patient: Pardon.

Doctor: There's nothing to worry about.

Patient: Nothing to worry about! It's all very well for you to say that. You'd be worried if you were going deaf at 30. I'd like to see you do your job if you couldn't hear what people said to you.

Doctor: (*loudly*) Mrs Cumberbunch you are not going deaf.

Patient: Not deaf?

Doctor: No. At least I very much doubt it. I'm going to write a prescription for some drops which I want you to put in your ears twice a day. Then come back in a fortnight and we'll see if we can get rid of all that wax.

Patient: Did you say drops?

Doctor: Yes. Look I'll write it down for you.

Patient: Oh thank you doctor.

➡ Copy out this table for each patient and make short notes under these headings on their Medical Record Card.

Name:		
Signs of illness	**Doctor's opinion**	**Treatment**
−2 red circular marks on left arm − Grey in middle − Been growing in size		

75

Unit 8: Keeping a diary

Erica's diary

These extracts tell the story of a girl who ran away from home.

Saturday 7 March

Today was the first day of my freedom. I left home at eleven o'clock with a sleeping bag, two pairs of jeans, three sweatshirts, five pairs of socks, six pairs of pants, one pair of shoes, a jacket, an acoustic guitar, a packet of biscuits, an apple and a carton of milk. I drank the milk and ate six biscuits on the train to London. Arrived at Kings Cross station at two o'clock. Police and football supporters everywhere. No-one noticed me.

1 When did Erica run away?
2 What time did she arrive at King's Cross station?
3 Why wasn't she noticed at the station?
4 What do you notice about the way her diary is written?

Keeping a diary means choosing to write down some of the things that happened to you and what you felt about them. You do not need to write in complete sentences.

Sunday 8 March

Last night was freezing! I couldn't sleep at all, even with all my clothes on in the sleeping bag. Found a good place though— the South Bank, above the National Theatre. Lots of other dossers there, young and old. Smells awful. Now what? Some of them are in a terrible state—filthy and really ill. I mustn't get like that.

Monday 9 March

Another freezing night. Must get some cardboard boxes like the others. Went round cafes looking for jobs. One bloke said I stank. Went to public baths for a shower. Felt marvellous. Money won't last long. Saw some of the others picking up fruit after the market.

Tuesday 10 March

Thought about home today. How easy it would be to go back. Warm and comfortable. What would they say? I'm half asleep all the time. Tried for jobs again. Not a hope. Met a French bloke outside an amusement arcade. First friendly voice I've heard in days. Offered me some cider. Said I should go to France and pick grapes. Drank half a bottle each then a policeman appeared. Took fright and ran. He might have asked questions.

Wednesday 11 March

Tried singing in the underground. Trouble is I only know two songs all the way through. Sang them over and over again. Got eighty seven pence. Then a guard threw me out.

Thursday 12 March

Woke up with a sore throat. Went busking down the underground again. Only managed to get thirty pence before two blokes turned up and said they always played there. Threatened to break my guitar if I didn't move. Sat on Circle Line tube and went to sleep. Woken up hours later by guard. Throat still hurt.

Friday 13 March

My throat is killing me. I can't stand this anymore. I'm going home. Just enough money left for the fare. Wonder what mum and dad will say?

5 Match these pictures to the things that happened to Erica. Decide on which day each one happened.

Keeping a diary

1 Make a long list of everything that you can remember happening to you yesterday.
Example:

> 1. Woke up at 6.15 because the alarm went off early.
> 2. I brushed my teeth as normal.
> 3. Wore my new trainers.
> 4. Fed the cat.
> 5. Didn't have any breakfast because the milk hadn't arrived ...again!
> 6. etc.

2 Cross out anything on your list that you don't think is very interesting.

3 Underline the most important details and add comments on how you felt about them.

4 Now write out what you did yesterday in the form of a diary.
Example:
Give it a title.

> Rob's Diary

Start the day with a capital letter.

> Friday

Start the date and month with a capital letter.

> 15 January

5 Write our your diary for all of the last week.

6 Keep a diary for the next week.

A week in the life of Donna

Saturday 15 June–Friday 21 June

Instead I nearly broke my ankle.

The next day the swelling was down.

Bought a present for Sue.

Sue phoned in the evening. Parent trouble!

The party was going great until the gate-crashers arrived.

Of course parents do have their uses.

1 Choose two days from Donna's week and write them out as a diary. You can add things not in the cartoon if you think they are what Donna might have written.

Example:

Donna's diary

Saturday 15 June
Got up early to catch the bus into town. Called on Susan as normal. Started another day at the check out (groan!). I was talking to Susan when that creepy new manager told us to stop gossiping. He really likes showing off in front of the customers . . . . .

2 Imagine you are Sue's dad. It is Thursday and after discussing it with your wife you have decided you must stay for the party in case there is any trouble, even though this will upset Sue. Write out his diary for Thursday and Friday. Try to include the details you think a father would consider to be important.

3 It is the day after the party. Imagine you are Sue and ringing Donna to chat about your party. In pairs work out the conversation they might have had. You could make a tape-recording of it or write it out as a script.

A diary of courage

In 1912 Robert Scott, the great explorer, died on an expedition to the Antarctic. He had four friends with him: Oates, Wilson, Evans and Bowers. Scott kept a diary of his last days. As you read, try to imagine Scott's feelings as he and his men gradually run out of food and strength.

Wednesday March 7

A little worse, I fear. One of Oates' feet very bad this morning; he is wonderfully brave. We still talk of what we will do together at home.

We only made $6\frac{1}{2}$ miles yesterday. This morning in $4\frac{1}{2}$ hours we did just over 4 miles. We are 16 from our depot. If we only find the correct amount of food there and this surface continues, we may get to the next depot but not to One Ton Camp.

Thursday March 8 – Lunch

Worse and worse in morning; poor Oates' left foot can never last out. Wilson's feet giving trouble now, but this mainly because he gives so much help to others. We did $4\frac{1}{2}$ miles this morning and are now $8\frac{1}{2}$ miles from the depot – a ridiculously small distance to feel in difficulties. The great question is: What shall we find at the depot? If the dogs have visited it we may get along a good distance, but if there is too little fuel, God help us indeed. We are in a very bad way, I fear, in any case.

Saturday March 10

Things steadily downhill. Oates' foot worse. He has great courage and must know that he can never get through. He asked Wilson if he had a chance this morning, and of course Bill had to say he didn't know. In point of fact he has none. Apart from him, if he went under now, I doubt whether we could get through. With great care we might have a dog's chance, but no more. The weather conditions are awful, and our gear gets steadily more icy and difficult to manage.

Sunday March 11

Titus Oates is very near the end, one feels. What we or he will do, God only knows. We discussed the matter over breakfast; he is a brave fine fellow and understands the situation, but he practically asked for advice. Nothing could be said but to urge him to march as long as he could.

We have 7 days' food and should be about 55 miles from One Ton Camp tonight, $6\times7=42$, leaving us 13 miles short of our distance, even if things get no worse.

Monday March 12

We did 6.9 miles yesterday, under our necessary average. Things are left much the same, Oates not pulling much, and now with hands as well as feet pretty well useless. We did 4 miles this morning in 4 hours 20 minutes – we may hope for 3 this afternoon, $7\times6=42$. We shall be 47 miles from the depot. I doubt if we can possibly do it. The surface remains awful, the cold intense, and our physical condition running down. God help us! Not a breath of favourable wind for more than a week.

Wednesday March 14

No doubt about the going downhill, but everything going wrong for us. Yesterday we woke to a strong northerly wind with temp. $-37°$. Couldn't face it, so remained in camp till 2, then did $5\frac{1}{4}$ miles. We must go on, but now the making of every camp must be more difficult and dangerous. It must be near the end. Poor Oates got it again in the foot. I shudder to think what it will be like tomorrow. It is only with greatest pains the rest of us keep off frost-bites. No idea there could be temperatures like this at this time of year with such winds. Truly awful outside tent. Must fight it out to the last biscuit, but can't reduce the rations.

Friday March 16, or Saturday 17

Lost track of dates, but think the last correct. Disaster all along the line. At lunch, the day before yesterday, poor Titus Oates said he couldn't go on; he said we should leave him in his sleeping-bag. That we could not do, and we persuaded him to come on, on the afternoon march. In spite of its awful nature for him he struggled on and we made a few miles. At night he was worse and we knew the end had come.

Should this be found I want these facts recorded. Oates' last thoughts were of his mother. We all admired his bravery. He has had great suffering for weeks without complaint, and to the very end was able and willing to discuss outside subjects. He did not – would not – give up hope till the very end. He was a brave soul. This was the end. He slept through the night before last, hoping not to wake; but he woke in the morning – yesterday. It was blowing a blizzard. He said, 'I am just going outside and may be some time.' He went out into the blizzard and we have not seen him since.

Sunday March 18

Today, lunch, we are 21 miles from the depot. My right foot has gone, nearly all the toes – two days ago I was the owner of two feet. Bowers takes first place in condition, but there is not much to choose after all. The others are still confident of getting through – or pretend to be – I don't know.

Monday March 19

Today we started in the usual dragging manner. Sledge dreadfully heavy. We are 15½ miles from the depot and ought to get there in three days. What progress! We have two days' food but barely a day's fuel. All our feet are getting bad – Wilson's best, my right foot worse, left all right. There is no chance to nurse one's feet till we can get hot food into us. Amputation is the least I can hope for now, but will the trouble spread?

Wednesday March 21

Got within 11 miles of depot Monday night; had to lay up all yesterday in severe blizzard.

22 and 23

Blizzard bad as ever – tomorrow last chance – no fuel and only one or two of food left – must be near the end. Have decided it shall be natural – we shall march for the depot and die in our tracks.

Thursday March 29

Since the 21st we have had a continuous gale. We had fuel to make two cups of tea apiece and bare food on the 20th. Every day we have been ready to start for our depot 11 miles away, but outside the door of the tent it remains a scene of whirling drift. I do not think we can hope for any better things now. We shall stick it out to the end, but we are getting weaker, of course, and the end cannot be far.

It seems a pity, but I do not think I can write more.

(adapted)

depot = base
blizzard = strong wind
amputation = cutting off an arm or a leg

The secret diary of Adrian Mole

> If you want to describe one day in great detail you can break it up by using the time in the same way that you normally use the date on a diary.

Class Four-D's trip to the British Museum

This is what happened to Class Four-D on their trip to the British Museum in London.

7. *a.m.* Boarded coach.
7.05 Ate packed lunch, drank low-calorie drink.
7.10 Coach stopped for Barry Kent to be sick.
7.20 Coach stopped for Claire Neilson to go to the Ladies.
7.30 Coach left school drive.
7.35 Coach returned to school for Ms Fossington-Gore's handbag.
7.40 Coach driver observed to be behaving oddly.
7.45 Coach stopped for Barry Kent to be sick again.
7.55 Approached motorway.
8.00 Coach driver stopped coach and asked everyone to stop giving 'V' signs to lorry drivers.
8.10 Coach driver loses temper, refuses to drive on motorway until 'bloody teachers control kids'.
8.20 Ms Fossington-Gore gets everyone sitting down.
8.25 Drive on to motorway.
8.30 Everyone singing 'Ten Green Bottles'.
8.35 Everyone singing 'Ten Green Snotrags'.
8.45 Coach driver stops singing by shouting very loudly.

9.15 Coach driver pulls in at service station and is observed to drink heavily from hip-flask.
9.30 Barry Kent hands round bars of chocolate stolen from self-service shop at service station. Ms Fossington-Gore chooses Bounty bar.
9.40 Barry Kent sick in coach.
9.50 Two girls sitting near Barry Kent are sick.
9.51 Coach driver refuses to stop on motorway.
9.55 Ms Fossington-Gore covers sick in sand.
9.56 Ms Fossington-Gore sick as a dog.
10.30 Coach crawls along on hard shoulder, all other lanes closed for repairs.
11.30 Fight breaks out on back seat as coach approaches end of motorway.
11.45 Fight ends. Ms Fossington-Gore finds first-aid kit and sees to wounds. Barry Kent is punished by sitting next to driver.
11.50 Coach breaks down at Swiss Cottage.
11.55 Coach driver breaks down in front of AA man.
12.30 Class Four-D catch London bus to St Pancras.
1 *p.m.* Class Four-D walk from St Pancras through Bloomsbury.
1.15 Ms Fossington-Gore knocks on door of Tavistock House, asks if Dr Laing will give Barry Kent a quick going-over. Dr Laing in America on lecture tour.
1.30 Enter British Museum. Adrian Mole and Pandora Braithwaite struck by evidence of World Culture. Rest of class Four-D run berserk, laughing at nude statues and dodging curators.
2.15 Ms Fossington-Gore in state of collapse. Adrian Mole makes reverse-charge phone call to headmaster. Headmaster in dinner lady strike-meeting, can't be disturbed.

1 Imagine you are Adrian Mole. You are very worried about what is going on in the British Museum. You try to ring the headmaster. You try to persuade the School Secretary to let you speak to him. Copy and complete this telephone conversation in pairs. You could record it.

OPERATOR: You're through now, Mr. Mole, go ahead.

ADRIAN M: Hello! Is that the headmaster?

SECRETARY: No, it's ....

ADRIAN M: Could I speak to the headmaster, please?

SECRETARY: Who are you?

ADRIAN M: ....

SECRETARY: What are you doing?

ADRIAN M: We're ....

SECRETARY: Well, why are you ringing?

ADRIAN M: ....

....

SECRETARY: I'm afraid you can't speak to the

headmaster he's ....

ADRIAN M: Look this is very important. If you

don't do something quickly ....

....

SECRETARY: Why are you ringing and not ....?

ADRIAN M: She's ....

SECRETARY: Well as I've said, I can't disturb him

now but I'll tell him that you rang. Now go

back to .... and tell her ....

....

3 p.m. Curators round up class Four-D and make them sit on steps of museum.

3.05 American tourists photograph Adrian Mole saying he is a 'cute English schoolboy'.

3.15 Ms Fossington-Gore recovers and leads class Four-D on sightseeing tour of London.

4 p.m. Barry Kent jumps in fountain at Trafalgar Square, as predicted by Adrian Mole.

4.30 Barry Kent disappears, last seen heading towards Soho.

4.35 Police arrive, take Four-D to mobile police unit, arrange coach back. Phone parents about new arrival time. Phone headmaster at home. Claire Neilson has hysterical fit. Pandora Braithwaite tells Ms Fossington-Gore she is a disgrace to teaching profession. Ms Fossington-Gore agrees to resign.

2 Imagine you are Ms Fossington-Gore. Copy and continue this letter that she wrote to the headmaster. Make sure you explain exactly why you can't face teaching any more, especially after such a terrible day.

Saturday 19 September

Dear Mr. Scruton,

I have just had the most terrible day of my teaching career. As you know I took Class 4-D to the British Museum. It was a disaster. I have never seen such badly behaved pupils.

Describe the day in brief. ——— To start with .....

I think Barry Kent .....

Continue this ——— I did my best to make this a good day, but I have no alternative to giving you my resignation. I regret any bad publicity this may bring the school.

Yours sincerely

B. Fossington-Gore.

Ms. Fossington-Gore

POLICE OFFICER: I am charging you with dangerous driving.

COACH DRIVER: But ....

POLICE OFFICER: I must warn you that anything you say now will be taken down and may be used in evidence against you.

COACH DRIVER: I don't care! My driving days are over anyway. I've never ever had such an awful group of kids. I'd only been going for ten minutes when ....

6 p.m. Barry Kent found in sex shop. Charged with theft of 'grow-it-big' cream and two 'ticklers'.

7 p.m. Coach leaves police station with police escort.

7.30 Police escort waves goodbye.

7.35 Coach driver begs Pandora Braithwaite to keep order.

7.36 Pandora Braithwaite keeps order.

8 p.m. Ms Fossington-Gore drafts resignation.

8.30 Coach driver afflicted by motorway madness.

8.40 Arrive back. Tyres burning. Class Four-D struck dumb with terror. Ms Fossington-Gore led off by Mr Scruton. Parents up in arms. Coach driver charged by police.

3 The police who have driven back with the coach from London arrest the driver. This is part of the conversation that took place between the driver and the police officer. Copy and complete it.

POLICE OFFICER: Excuse me sir, are you the driver of this coach?

COACH DRIVER: Y-Yes I am!

The next day

4 The headmaster held a special assembly for all those who had been on the school trip. What would you have said if you were in his position? In pairs, make a list of all the things you think went wrong. Use the list to plan the very short speech you would have given to Class Four-D.

At a later date

5 In groups plan an outing to somewhere near your school.
   a) Make a list of all the possible places and choose one.
   b) Use a map to find out how far it is.
   c) Find out how much it costs and plan how much money each person should take.
   d) Work out a timetable for the day and write it out.
   e) Agree a list of five simple pieces of advice for students and teachers who are going on a school trip.
   (You could use Adrian Mole's diary to help you.)

6 Write your own secret diary of the school trip you have just planned. If you like, it could go wrong too. Set it out like the diary you have just read.

Recording your progress in English:
Record Sheet 2

Name:

Date of recording:

I can:	:)	:)	:(	My comments
write a simple script				
choose material				
write a personal letter				
set out an envelope				
write simple messages				
make a list				
make notes				
set out a diary				
keep a diary for a week				
write in paragraphs				
read aloud				
respond to reading				
listen to others' opinions				
listen to a simple message				
give opinions in a group				
take decisions in a group				

Unit 9: Writing out speech

1 In this cartoon story four of the balloons have been left blank. Decide what should go in the balloons and write it down.

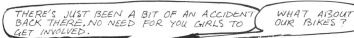

2 Copy the chart below and fill in the spaces with your own words.

	Speaker	What is actually said
a		Wow, Clio, this telescope is amazing!...
b		What is it?
c		
d		It's going to land somewhere near here...
e		Let's get our bikes and look for it...
f		I'm tired, Zoya. Maybe it was just a...
g		
h		Sorry girls, no-one's allowed past this point.
i		But why not?
j		You girls shouldn't be out this late.
k		There's no law against cycling at night.
l		
m		But we don't want a lift home.
n		There's just been a bit of an accident...
o		What about our bikes?
p		We'll arrange for someone to bring them round.
q		Nothing to worry about Mrs. de Silva...
r		
s		Space-ship! You kids have been watching too much T.V....

3 Read the script aloud with a partner. Take each part in turn.

4 When you are sure who is speaking add the name to the left-hand side of your chart.
Example:

Speaker	What is actually said
Zoya	Wow Clio, this telescope is amazing!...

You now have a script like the ones you read in Unit 5 (pages 46–53).

5 Use the cartoon and your chart to turn this into a story. In pairs tell your idea of the story to each other. This is how the story starts:

Late one evening Zoya and Clio were sitting in their bedroom. Zoya was looking through a telescope, when suddenly a strange shape appeared. It looked like some kind of spaceship....

Writing out speech in a story

When you write out a story there are often moments when you will want to include what your characters say.

There are four simple rules to remember for writing out speech. Read them and then copy them out.

Rule 1 You put speech marks ('   ') at the beginning and end of *what is actually said*.

Rule 2 The *first* word spoken starts with a capital letter.

Rule 3 Each time a *different* person starts speaking you begin a new line *as if* you were starting a new paragraph.

Rule 4 Before the *last* set of speech marks (') you must have one of the following:
   a) a full stop   .
   b) a comma   ,
   c) an exclamation mark   !
   d) a question mark   ?

Example:

Late one night

Late one evening Zoya and Clio were sitting in their bedroom. Zoya said,
  'Wow Clio, this telescope is amazing! You can see all kinds of things. Hey – wait a minute.'
  'What is it?' Clio asked.

In the story so far there are two different words used for speaking:

  a) Zoya said.   **b)** Clio asked.

You may want to use other words when you write up the story. Here are some more words to help you:
  c) shout
  d) answer
  e) reply
  f) scream
  g) enquire.

If you are not sure what these words mean, look them in up the dictionary at the back of the book.

➡ Use the chart you made to help you write out the story. Remember the four rules.

Two friends make up

Look carefully at this picture and try to work out what has happened.

Joby walked faster, kicking at loose stones lying in the lane.

'Wait on,' Snap said.

Joby ignored him.

Snap caught him up. 'Wait on, Joby. Where you going?'

Joby said nothing.

'Don't get mad, Joby,' Snap said. He put his arm across Joby's shoulder and Joby shrugged impatiently under its weight.

'Come on, Joby. Don't get mad.'

'I'm not mad.'

'Y'are. I can see y'are.'

'I'll get mad if you keep saying I'm mad.'

'OK, you're not mad.'

'What if I am mad, anyway? What's it to do with you?'

'I don't want you to be mad with me. We're mates, aren't we?'

Well you could get mad easily with Snap, but you couldn't stay mad with him for long. Joby reached up and took Snap's hand, pulling Snap's arm round his shoulders.

'OK, we're mates.'

from *Joby* by Stan Barstow

1 In pairs read aloud what Joby and Snap say to each other. *Remember:* These will be the words in speech marks.

2 What do you think happened before this? What made Joby mad? Make up something that could have happened just before we hear Joby and Snap speaking.

Write it out using description and speech. Finish with the first sentence of the extract above: *Joby walked faster, kicking at loose stones lying in the lane.* Give your writing a title.

89

The last train

by *Brian Keaney*

Scene 1

A platform in a London Underground station late at night. **Mick** *walks along the platform. He is about twenty. His clothes are torn and filthy. His hair is wild and matted. He looks as if he sleeps rough.*

> (**Mick** *goes up to a middle-aged man, who is carrying a rolled up umbrella and reading a folded newspaper.*)

Mick: Got any spare change?

Man: I beg your pardon?

Mick: Got any spare change mate? Just something to help pay the rent.

Man: Don't you know that begging is against the law?

Mick: You what mate? Ain't you got fifty pence just to help me get something to eat?

Man: No I haven't. I work too damn hard for my money to give it away to people like you.

Mick: Well you're lucky, ain't you? I ain't got a job.

Man: I'm not surprised. Who do you think would employ you, looking like that?

Mick: Nobody. That's what I'm telling you. Come on, ain't you even got ten pence?

Man: No I have not. Now clear off before I call a guard.

Mick: You call a guard. See what happens.

Man: Are you threatening me?

Mick: Yeah.

> (*The* **man** *walks briskly away.* **Mick** *moves on.*)

Scene 2

> (**Mick** *walks up to two young women who are standing talking.*)

Mick: Got any spare change?

Susan: Did he say something?

Maureen: I don't know.

Mick: You got any spare change? Just something to help pay the rent.

Susan: Are you one of those glue sniffers?

Maureen: I bet he is. He looks right out of his head.

Susan: You just want the money to buy drugs, don't you?

Mick: Ain't you got fifty pence just to help me get something to eat?

Susan: Do you think we should give him something, Maureen?

Maureen: You can if you like. I'm not.

Susan: Here.

Mick: Ten pence. Ain't you got a bit more?

Susan: Didn't anybody ever teach you any manners? You're supposed to say thank you when somebody gives you something.

Mick: I haven't had any food since yesterday.

Susan: Well! I've only had a yogurt, half a tomato and a bit of lettuce since this morning. And the yogurt tasted off.

Maureen: You want to pull yourself together. Look at the state you're in. You're filthy. You smell. Don't you care?

Mick: Ain't you got any more change?

SUSAN: No I have not. Go and try somewhere else.

> (**Mick** *moves on.*)

Scene 3

(**Mick** *walks up to a Tourist who is standing on his own.*)

Mick: Got any spare change?

Tourist: Sorry. I don't understand. I speak only a little English.

Mick: Got any money?

Tourist: Money. For what?

Mick: Just something to help pay the rent.

Tourist: Sorry. Can you speak more slowly please. I have only a little English.

Mick: I want some money.

Tourist: Yes, I understand. But why? I have not much money.

Mick: I haven't eaten since yesterday.

Tourist: You want money to eat?

Mick: That's right, yeah. I need money to eat.

Tourist: Wait. I will see what I have got.

(*He puts his hand in his pocket and brings out a handful of notes and coins.* **Mick's** *eyes light up. At the same moment the middle-aged man with the rolled umbrella arrives with a Guard.*)

Man: There he is. Still at it.

Guard: Come on then mate, out of the station. (*to* **Tourist**) I should put your money away if I was you, sir.

Tourist: Sorry. I don't understand. I speak only a little English.

Guard: Are you coming or are we going to have to get the law down here?

Mick: You got any spare change. Just something to help pay the rent?

Guard: Course I haven't. If I had I wouldn't be working here. Now shift or else.

(*The* **Guard** *takes* **Mick** *by the arm and begins to lead him out of the station.* **Mick** *does not struggle.*)

Man: Well that sorted him out. They're all the same. Plenty of talk, but when it comes to the showdown, nothing to back it up.

Tourist: Sorry, can you speak more slowly please. I have only a little English.

Man: Oh never mind.

(*The last train arrives in the station.*)

1 Choose one of these scenes and write it out as a story with speech. You will need to add to what Brian Keaney has written.

Example:

Use the information from the script to help you write your opening paragraph.

You can add details from what is suggested in the script.

THE LAST TRAIN

It is late at night on a London Underground Station.

A man called Mick is walking along the platform. His clothes are torn and filthy and his hair is wild and matted. He looks about twenty, but it is difficult to be sure how old he is because of his appearance. He looks as if he sleeps rough.

Mick goes up to a middle-aged man, who is carrying a rolled up umbrella and reading a newspaper.

You could add another sentence of your own to describe the middle-aged man.

Use a word to introduce the speech of each person.

Mick asks him,
"Got any spare change?" The man doesn't hear him and replies,
"I beg your pardon?" Mick says again,
"Got any spare change mate? Just something to pay the rent."
"Don't you know that begging is against the law?"

Show who has spoken.

You don't always need to use a word to show someone is speaking if it's clear.

2 Continue the third scene in pairs. Imagine what the guard and Mick say to each other as Mick is led out of the station.

3 Make up a fourth scene and write it out as a story *or* script. Think of more people that Mick might meet in the Underground station.

Photo-speech

1 Here are three photographs taken *after* something has happened.
   a) Decide what happened *before* they were taken.
   b) Decide who the people are.
   c) Decide what their names are.

   d) Choose one of the pictures. In one or two paragraphs write the story behind it.
   e) Use as much speech as you can, set out as explained on page 93.

What would you say?

2 Here are four situations. Choose two of them and write a paragraph describing what happened next. Include speech and make what you say as realistic as possible.

Situation A You are invited to a birthday party. You don't know anyone. You stand at the edge watching people dancing. Then two people come over to you and start talking to you. . . .

Situation B You have found a ten-pound note in the street. You are just picking it up when a man rushes up the street towards you. He asks you if you've seen a wallet lying around. . . .

Situation C You have bought a record from a shop in the High Street. You take it home to play it and find that it has a scratch on one side. You take it back to the shop to complain. . . .

Situation D You have a friend who is being bullied at school but he is too scared to tell a teacher. You decide to take matters into your own hands and try and sort things out. . . .

The report

3 If you have ever had a bad report you will be sympathetic to the situation in this passage. Some of the speech has been left out and is jumbled up at the end. In pairs try and put it back in the right order.

What a rotten report. It was the worst report I'd ever had. I'd dreaded bringing it home for my mum to read. We were sitting at the kitchen table having our tea, but neither of us had touched anything. It was gammon and chips as well, with a pineapple ring. My favourite. We have gammon every Friday, because my Auntie Doreen works on the bacon counter at the Co-op, and she drops it in on her way home. I don't think she pays for it.

My mum was reading the report for the third time. She put it down on the table and stared at me. I didn't say anything. I just stared at my gammon and chips and pineapple ring. What could I say? My mum looked so disappointed. I really felt sorry for her. She was determined for me to do well at school, and get my 'O' Levels, then get my 'A' Levels, then go to university, then get my degree, and then get a good job with good prospects...

'I'm sorry, Mum...'

She picked up the report again, and started reading it for the fourth time.

'It's no good reading it again, Mum. It's not going to get any better.'

She slammed the report back on to the table.

_____**1**_____ I'm not in the mood for it.'

I hadn't meant it to be cheeky, but I suppose it came out like that.

'I wouldn't say anything if I was you, after reading this report!'

I shrugged my shoulders.

_____**2**_____

'You can tell me what went wrong. You told me you worked hard this term!'

I *had* told her I'd worked hard, but I hadn't.

_____**3**_____

'Not according to this.'

She waved the report under my nose.

'You're supposed to be taking your 'O' Levels next year. What do you think is going to happen then?'

I shrugged my shoulders again, and stared at my gammon and chips.

_____**4**_____

She put the report back on the table. I knew I hadn't done well in my exams because of everything that had happened this term, but I didn't think for one moment I'd come bottom in nearly everything. Even Norbert Lightowler had done better than me.

'You've come bottom in nearly everything. Listen to this.'

She picked up the report again.

'Maths – Inattentive and lazy.'

I knew what it said.

_____**5**_____

She leaned across the table, and put her face close to mine.

_____**6**_____

She didn't have to keep reading it.

'Well, stop reading it then.'

My mum just gave me a look.

by George Layton

A 'I did work hard, Mum.'
B 'Don't you make cheeky remarks to me.'
C 'I know what it says, Mum.'
D 'I know what it says too and I don't like it.'
E 'There's nothing much I can say, is there?'
F 'I don't know.'

Answers on page 105.

Unit 10: Understanding instructions

Giving instructions

How to mend a puncture

Read aloud and follow these instructions.

Use tyre levers to take one side of tyre off wheel.

Take inner tube out.

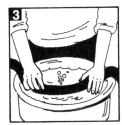
Put inner tube in bowl of water to find puncture.

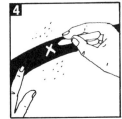
Dry inner tube and mark leak with chalk.

Select patch of right size.

Spread glue on tube and on patch.

After one minute stick patch and tube together.

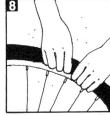
Put tube back in tyre and tyre back on wheel.

How to make an omelette

Copy and complete these instructions using the pictures to help you.

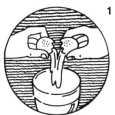
1 Break three eggs into a bowl.

2 _____

3 _____

4 _____

5 _____

6 _____

7 Serve omelette.

Telling a friend

P

In pairs, give clear instructions so that your partner could find out:
a) how to make a paper dart from a piece of paper
b) how to change the sheets on a bed
c) how to use a telephone
d) how to use a cassette recorder.

96

Unscrambling instructions

How to wire a plug

Here are some mixed-up instructions.
Use the pictures to help you put them in the right order.

➡ **a)** Put back of plug on again.
b) Take off back of plug with a screwdriver.
c) Check all five screws are done up tightly.
d) Loosen two screws at bottom of plug.
e) Put green/yellow wire in at the top.
f) Put blue wire in at the left.
g) Put brown wire in on right.
h) Feed wires into plug.

Warning!: If you really are going to change a plug then turn to page 105 and read the answers carefully.

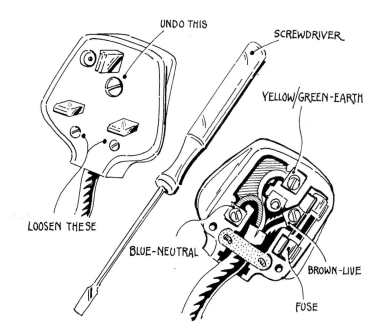

UNDO THIS

SCREWDRIVER

YELLOW/GREEN-EARTH

LOOSEN THESE

BLUE-NEUTRAL

BROWN-LIVE

FUSE

How to play volleyball

A friend of yours has just started playing a game called volleyball. When you ask how to play the game, this is what you are told. Read it aloud and then try to write some clear instructions. Use about 12 points and number them carefully.

'It's very simple really. Each side has six players. You play games on a pitch like a tennis court with a net in the middle. To start the game the server hits the ball with his/her hand to send it over the net. A player continues to serve until his or her team loses a point. When one team loses a point, the other team takes over the service. Everyone takes it in turns to serve. Each team can hit the ball three times on their side of the net before returning it. You can only win a point when you're serving. You win a point if the ball touches the ground on the other side of the net. A set is fifteen points and a match is the best of five sets. It's really very easy ... honest!'

Example:

> How to play volleyball
> 1. Each side has 6 players.

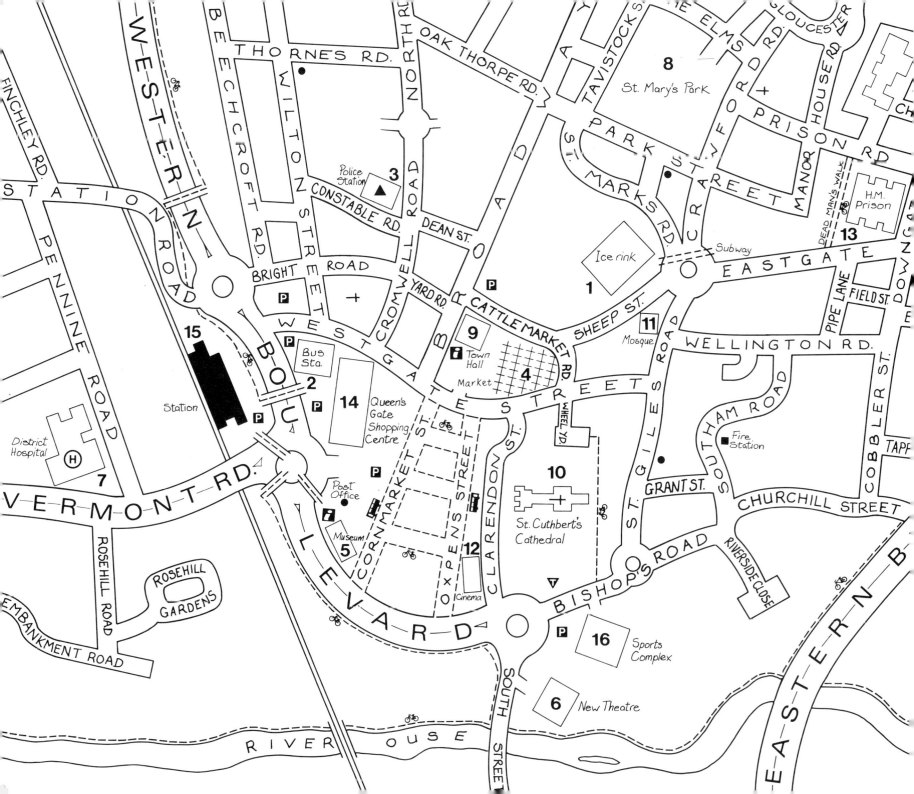

Finding your way

1 Find these places on the map and write down their numbers.

   a) Sports Complex
   b) Cathedral
   c) Cinema
   d) Railway Station
   e) Bus Station
   f) New Theatre
   g) Hospital
   h) Park
   i) Town Hall
   j) Police Station
   k) Mosque
   l) Market
   m) Prison
   n) Ice Rink
   o) Museum
   p) Shopping Centre

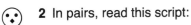

2 In pairs, read this script:

John: (*standing outside the Town Hall*) Excuse me! Could you tell me how to get to the New Theatre?

Amanda: Yes, it's not far. Turn left and walk down Broadway to Westgate Street. Turn left and the third street on the right is Clarendon Street. So you cross over and go down Clarendon Street – it's by the Cathedral. When you reach the roundabout go straight across to South Street. You'll see the theatre on your left by the river.

John: Thanks a lot!

P

3 In pairs, give clear directions to get to the Bus Station from these places:

   a) the Ice Rink
   b) the Police Station
   c) the Museum
   d) the Park.

4 Find these places:
   a) somewhere to buy fruit and vegetables
   b) somewhere to worship
   c) somewhere to go if you've broken your leg
   d) a place to watch a film.

5 Choose two of these places and write down a set of clear directions to get from one to the other.

6 Follow this tour and see where you end up!

Mystery Tour

Start at the Local History Museum. Go into Cornmarket Street. Take the first right into Church Street, then left into Oxpens Street. Turn right into Westgate Street, then take the second left into St. Giles Road. Take the first right into Wellington Road, then second left into Down Gate Road. Turn left into Prison Road, then second left into Crawford Road. When you reach the roundabout, go straight across into Sheep Street. What is the building to your right?

Answer on page 105.

A story poem

Mart was my best friend

Mart was my best friend.
I thought he was great,
but one day he tried to do for me.

I had a hat – a woolly one
and I loved that hat.
It was warm and tight.
My mum had knitted it
and I wore it everywhere.

One day me and Mart were out
and we were standing at a bus-stop
and suddenly
he goes and grabs my hat
and chucked it over the wall.
He thought I was going to go in there
and get it out.
He thought he'd make me do that
because he knew I liked that hat so much
I wouldn't be able to stand being without it.

Hc was right –
I could hardly bear it.
I was really scared I'd never get it back.
But I never let on.
I never showed it on my face.
I just waited.

'Aren't you going to get your hat?'
he says.
'Your hat's gone,' he says.
'Your hat's over the wall.'
I looked the other way.

But I could still feel on my head
how he had pulled it off.
'Your hat's over the wall,' he says.
I didn't say a thing.

Then the bus came round the corner
at the end of the road.

If I go home without my hat
I'm going to walk through the door
and Mum's going to say,
'Where's your hat?'
and if I say,
'It's over the wall,'
she's going to say,
'What's it doing there?'
and I'm going to say,
'Mart chucked it over,'
and she's going to say,
'Why didn't you go for it?'
and what am I going to say then?
What am I going to say then?

The bus was coming up.
'Aren't you going over for your hat?
There won't be another bus for ages,'
Mart says.

The bus was coming closer.
'You've lost your hat now,'
Mart says.

The bus stopped.
I got on
Mart got on
The bus moved off.

'You've lost your hat,' Mart says.

'You've lost your hat,' Mart says.

Two stops ahead, was ours.
'Are you going indoors without it?' Mart says.
I didn't say a thing.

The bus stopped.

Mart got up.
and dashed downstairs.
He'd got off one stop early.
I got off when we got to our stop.

Later,
I was drinking some orange juice.
The front door-bell rang.
It was Mart.
He had the hat in his hand.
He handed it me – and went.

I shut the front door –
put on the hat
and walked into the kitchen.
Mum looked up.
'You don't need to wear your hat indoors do you?'
she said.
'I will for a bit,' I said.
And I did.

by *Mike Rosen*

I went home
walked through the door
'Where's your hat?' Mum says.
'Over a wall,' I said.
'What's it doing there?' she says.
'Mart chucked it over there,' I said.
'But you haven't left it there, have you?' she says.
'Yes,' I said.
'Well don't you ever come asking me to make you
anything like that again.
You make me tired, you do.'

▧ Follow these instructions to write your own story-poem.

1 Write a very short story in one or two paragraphs.

2 Split up all your sentences into short groups of words.
Example:

Life/was really rough/the day I met Flynn.

3 Copy out your sentences like Mike Rosen has.

 4 Read your story-poem.

A recipe poem

How to make fish tea

It's easy.
You need for one person,
one nice fresh fish.
Not one that was a long time on the stall.
A small fish that will only make you one cup.
Clean the fish well
and wash it in a lot of water.
Then put a small pot on with
one and a half cupfuls of water,
a little pepper, one onion chopped,
a little thyme, one peg of garlic and the fish.
A bay leaf brings out your flavour
so that you don't need salt, not much.
Add a little butter.
Simmer for five minutes on a low fire.
The less water, the more you enjoy it.
For more than one person
add a cup for each and a fish.
Lovely!

Instructions

1 Using some of the instructions you have made in this unit, or a recipe that you know, write a poem that tells someone how to make something.
2 Remove the numbers from your instructions.
3 You can start your poem with *It's easy*.

A shape poem

Look at the way Roger McGough has spread these words over the page.

Watchwords

watch the words
watch words the
watchword is
watch words are
sly as boots
ifyoutakeyoureyesoffthemforaminute

up

and   they're   and

away

allover

the

place

by *Roger McGough*

Choose one of these ideas, or think of your own, and follow the instructions.

a) falling off a cliff   e) table
b) wings   f) fork
c) rain   g) hands
d) tennis

Instructions

1 Think of a shape of your own.
2 Draw the shape in pencil.
3 Cover it with words.
4 Write out your poem using these ideas.

A name poem

 Look at this carefully and work out who wrote the poem.

Bill
Is my name
Luckily enough
Loads of other people have a name

Like mine
Unluckily some
Car headlights
Also
Share part of it!

Follow these instructions and try to write your own name poem.

1 Write your name down the left-hand side of the paper.
2 Start each line of your poem with a letter from your name.
3 Fill up your poem with words that say something about you.
4 Don't worry if it's not serious.
5 Write it out neatly.

A 'parents-always-know-best' poem

Don't interrupt!

Turn the television down!
None of your cheek!
Sit down!
Shut up!
Don't make a fool of yourself!
Respect your elders!
I can't put up with you anymore!
Go outside.
Don't walk so fast!
Don't run.
Don't forget to brush your teeth!
Don't forget to polish your shoes!
Don't slam the door!
Have manners!
Don't interrupt when I'm talking!......

        x   x   x

Don't shout!
Don't listen to my conversation.
Don't look at the sun it could blind you.
Don't bite your nails!
Don't suck your thumb!
Why don't you answer me!
You never listen to a word I say!
Don't interrupt when I'm talking!

From *Don't interrupt* by *Demetroulla Vassili*

Note: The x x x shows that the middle part of this poem has been missed out.

  1 Think up some of the things that your parents are always telling you.

   Either **a)** Copy out the rest of this poem and fill your lines in the middle

     or **b)** Make up a poem out of your own lines.

How to survive at school

1 Decide which of these bags would be most useful to you and why.

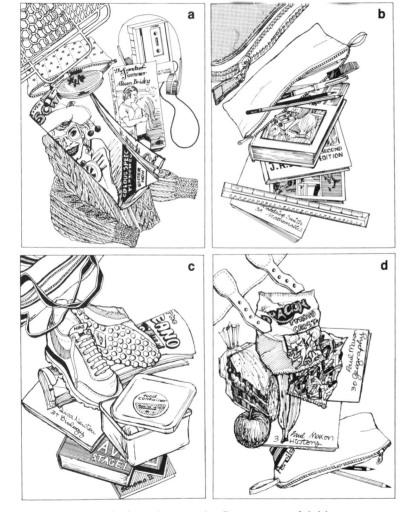

2 In groups decide what are the five most useful things to take to school. Make a list. Be prepared to back up your choices.

3 Study this map of a typical school.

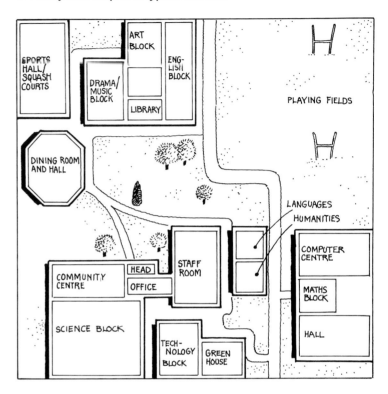

4 Make a map of your own school. Include:
  a) a sports hall
  b) the library
  c) the headteacher's office
  d) the school office
  and anything else you think is important.

5 *In another colour*, add
  a) where you register
  b) where you have lunch
  c) where you go during break-time
  d) any other places of your choice.

6 In a different colour, mark the five most important places that any new student to the school should know about.

7 Something has gone wrong with the plan for this typical school day. Read it carefully and put it back into the right order:

11.20–12.20	Third lesson
2.00– 3.00	Last lesson
3.10	Catch bus home
8.15	Catch bus to school
8.45– 9.00	Morning Registration
8.30	Arrive at school
12.20– 2.00	Lunch
9.00–10.00	First lesson
11.00–11.20	Morning break
10.00–11.00	Second lesson

8 Make a plan to give to anyone new to your school to help them get through a typical day.
Add your own tips too.

9 Here are some drawings of some of the different kinds of people who work in a school.

Give each one a name and decide what they do. Think up other details about them:
a) how old they are
b) where they live
c) what they like
d) what they don't like
e) what their hobbies are.
For each one, write a short description. You can set it out like this:

Name:	Likes:
Address:	
	Dislikes:
Age:	
Occupation:	Hobbies:

Answers

A The report (page 95) = **B, E, A, F, C, D**.
B How to wire a plug (page 97) = **B, D, H, E, F, G, C, A**.
C Mystery Tour (page 99) = Ice Rink.

105

Unit 11: Finding things out

a $\alpha\beta\gamma\delta\epsilon\zeta$

Alphabets

1 Do you know which
languages these letters
come from?
(Answer on page 127.)

b

c جخذزرزذج d аӧвгд

The first two letters in example **a** are called 'alpha' and
'beta'. This is how we came to have the word 'alphabet' to
describe the letters in the Roman and Greek alphabets.

There are 26 letters in the Roman alphabet. The Hindi
alphabet has 46 letters.

2 Here is the Roman alphabet in capital letters.
ABCDEFGHIJKLMNOPQRSTUVWXYZ
Write the alphabet in small letters. (Some alphabets, like
Hindi and Arabic, do not have capital letters.)

3 These letters are called vowels.
Aa Ee Ii Oo Uu
Most words have at least one vowel.

4 With a partner decide which of these statements is correct.
a) The letter **v** comes after **u**.
b) **Q** and **q** are the same letter.
c) **D** and **b** are the same letter.
d) 23 letters of the alphabet are not vowels.
e) The word alphabet comes from Greece.
f) There are no vowels in the last five letters of the
alphabet.
g) **L** comes after **m**.
h) **U** and **u** are not the same letter.
i) All alphabets are the same.

Alphabetical order

It helps us to find things more easily if they are in alphabetical
order. This means putting all the words which begin with the
same letter together, and then ordering them from A to Z.

Example: banana   apple   cake   dog

If we put these words into alphabetical order, the order is:
apple
banana
cake
dog

1 Put these words into alphabetical order based on their first
letter:
bicycle   hovercraft   car   aeroplane

If there is more than one word with the same first letter, you
will need to look at the second or third letter as well.

Example: boat   bicycle   bus

– each word starts with the letter **b**
– the second letters of the words are **o i u** so they become

bicycle   **bo**at   **bu**s

2 Put these words into alphabetical order:

tourist   temple   ten   top
thimble   taste   too

In registers, telephone-directories, street directories, class
lists, and many other lists, names are listed alphabetically.

Example: John *Andrews*, Robert *James*, Jane *Button*
would be
John **A**ndrews
Jane **B**utton
Robert **J**ames

3 Put these names into alphabetical order and write them out
in a list:
John Smith, Paula Eustace, Janet Draper, Salima Ali,
Wayne Davies, Samantha Williamson, Karen Moon,
Bill Dixon, Mark West, Kamala Patel.

Using a dictionary

Using a dictionary is one way of finding out for yourself about words. Dictionaries are set out in alphabetical order.

Meaning

You can find out what words mean by looking in a dictionary.
Example:

A
accent – way of pronouncing words
address – name of place where letters are directed
advertisement – public notice, e.g. in newspaper or on television
announce – make something known, say something publicly
anxious – nervous, troubled, uneasy
appalled – shocked, dismayed, horrified
assure – tell confidently, confirm, convince

B
berserk – mad, furious, wild
blank – empty, not filled in
blaze – flame, fire
botanic garden – place where plants are grown and studied
briskly – quickly

 Follow this flowchart.

1 Don't know what a word means

2 Look it up in a dictionary

3 Find the first, second letter, etc.

4 Choose a meaning that fits the word

5 Check that your new word or words work.

1 Look up the meanings of the words in **bold** below in the example opposite. Write down their meanings.
   a) The girl had a northern **accent**.
   b) I lit a match and the bonfire became a **blaze**.
   c) I took my aunt to the **Botanic Gardens** to see some unusual flowers.
   d) The dog had been locked up for so long that it went **berserk** when I let it free.
   e) I am **appalled** at this terrible behaviour.

2 Using the dictionary in this book on pages 126–127, look up these words. Make up a sentence for each one to show that *you* can use them.
   a) prey   e) guilty
   b) emergency   f) castor-oil
   c) talkative   g) satellite
   d) strap

   Example: My dad is so **talkative** that I can never get a word in edgeways.

3 Using a school dictionary, do the same for these words.
   a) fond   d) enamel
   b) postpone   e) cackle
   c) stagger   f) vein

Spelling

You can use a dictionary to check how words are spelt.

1 Use the dictionary on pages 126–127 to check the spellings of the words in bold in these sentences:
   a) My mother was **apalled** at the state of my room.
   b) I'm much more **confidant** now I've started doing drama.
   c) The prisoner was found **giulty**.
   d) There was a long **pawse** while I changed my mind.
   e) When I picked up the **reciever** there was a strange clicking sound.
   f) Our new home has only one **story**.
   g) I like the new shops in the **precict**.
   h) My dad brought us back a **mangoe** to try.

Crosswords

You can use a dictionary to help with puzzles and crosswords. Use the dictionary in this book to help you fill in this crossword.

Across
 1 small shed
 3 close
 6 what Mr O'Riordan had in unit 7
10 tidily

Down
 2 lines of people
 4 close
 5 a play written out
 7 kind of oil used as medicine
 8 soldier on guard
 9 somebody you don't know

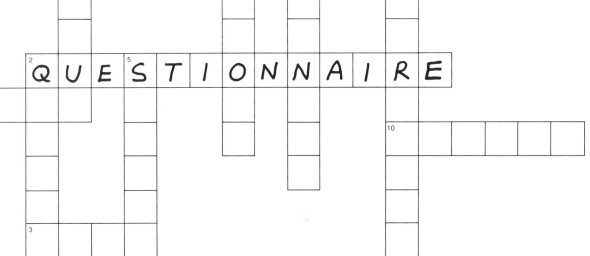

Finding out from books

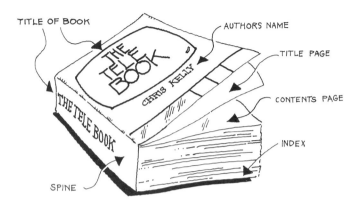

1 Who wrote this book?
2 What do you call a person who writes books?
3 What is the title of this book?
4 Where can you find out what is in a book?

Look at this piece of a Contents page.
1 What kind of book do you think it came from? Why?

2 Make up a title for the book.

CONTENTS

The library

One of the best places to find out more for yourself is in the school or local library.

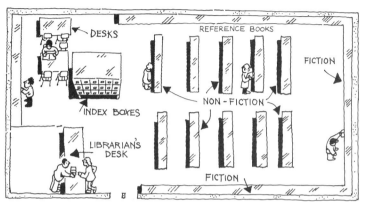

Librarian – person in charge of library
Fiction – stories
Non-fiction – books about different subjects, e.g. animals, sports, other countries, travel, etc.
Index – where you look up books
Reference books – books like dictionaries, encyclopedias, etc.

1 Draw a map of your school library. Label it like the diagram above.

2 Use this questionnaire to find out more about your library. Copy it out and fill it in.
Example:

Name of school ....
Name of librarian or teacher ....
How do you take a book out? ....
....
How long can you have a book out for? ....
How do you find the book you want? ....
....
Make a list of your hobbies and interests and the names of books about them

HOBBY   BOOK TITLE

Mysteries

The mystery of the Bermuda Triangle

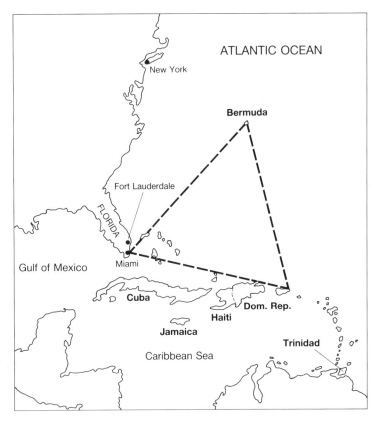

One of the most frightening areas of the world is a small part of the Atlantic Ocean known as the Bermuda Triangle. In this triangle of sea more than one hundred ships and planes have disappeared without trace. More than a thousand people have lost their lives here. Yet the strangest fact of all is that from all these ships and planes there haven't been any bodies or pieces of wreckage found. Although the area has been carefully searched, a frightening number of people have simply sunk without trace into the sea.

On December 5, 1945, five Avenger bombers, Flight 19, left Fort Lauderdale Naval Air Station in the United States of America. They were on a normal training flight and planned to fly along the triangle marked on the map. It was a fine day with the sun shining and only a few clouds. All the planes were in excellent condition, had full tanks of fuel and plenty of radio equipment to allow them to talk to each other. Each plane carried a life-raft and all the men wore life-jackets.

At 3.15 pm something began to go terribly wrong. The leader of the mission sent out an emergency message.

'Calling tower ... this is an emergency ... we seem to be off course ... we cannot see land ... we are not sure of our position ... everything's wrong ... we can't be sure of any direction ... even the ocean doesn't look as it should ...'

The leader's name was Lieutenant Charles Taylor. He had over 2,500 hours of flying experience. But no amount of experience could help him or the rest of Flight 19. Somehow they just disappeared.

Back at the base there was panic. Already that day something unusual had happened. One of the flight crew had refused to fly because he was afraid something was going to happen. Immediately they sent out another plane to look for them. A flying boat called a Martin Mariner took off with a large crew and all the rescue equipment it needed. It couldn't find them. At 4.00 pm the flying boat sent back this message.

'We are not sure where we are ... we think we must be 225 miles north-east of base ... it looks like we are.'

That was the last they heard from it. In one day 27 men and six planes and 21 ships went out to search the area but nothing was ever found. So began the mystery of the Bermuda Triangle.

Much later in 1974 some more strange evidence came to light. A reporter who had been studying the case said that he had found out what the last message from the flying boat had really been. It was...

'Don't come after me ... they look like they're from outer space.'

Since 1945 there have been many other strange disappearances. In 1947 a C.54 plane disappeared leaving only some seat cushions and an oxygen bottle which may not even have been from the plane. In 1948 a small boat, 'Al Snider', vanished without trace. In 1969 'The Teignmouth Electron' was found abandoned. It had been taking part in 'The Sunday

Times'-around-the-world-race and doing very well. Mysteriously it was found empty and drifting with everything in reasonably good order. There was two days' worth of dirty washing-up and enough food. The radios on the ship looked as if they had been taken apart. The life-raft was firmly in place on the deck. There was no apparent reason why anyone should have left the boat. Yet Donald Crowhurst, its owner and sailor, was never found. He came from Somerset in England. Had he cracked up under the strain or was he the victim of something more sinister? To this day no one knows.

Many ideas have been put forward to explain these and all the many other strange disappearances. Some people think there are huge sea-monsters in this area. Some think it has something to do with the large number of U.F.O.s seen in this part of the Atlantic. Perhaps the Bermuda Triangle is like a Black Hole into which things are sucked and destroyed.

Whatever suggestions are made there are still a number of unanswered questions:

(1) Why have so many planes and ships disappeared in such a small area at times when the weather has been good?

(2) Why have radios and compasses behaved strangely?

(3) Why has nothing ever been found from all these disappearances?

Find out more about this mystery. These are some books you could read:

The Bermuda Triangle by Charles Berlitz
The Bermuda Triangle by John Simkin
Without Trace by John Harris
The Secrets of the Bermuda Triangle by Alan Landsbury

Some notes about the monster's history

April 1933:   Mr and Mrs John McKay driving by the loch, say they saw an enormous monster.

December 1933: First photo taken.

April 1934:   R. K. Wilson took photo opposite.

1960:   Tim Dinsdale took film showing large object moving across the loch.

1962:   Loch Ness Phenomena Investigation Bureau set up – used submarine and gyrocopter – didn't find anything.

1933–now: Many sightings – normally of a humped animal with neck – animal makes waves on surface – moves very fast – tends to appear when few people around.

The Loch Ness monster

Read this information about another famous mystery and then decide what you think about it.

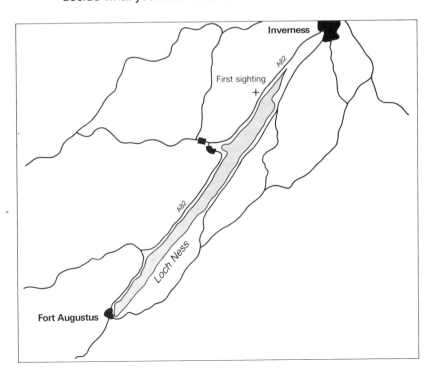

1 *On your own*, decide what you think about the monster based on this very small amount of evidence.

2 In a group, talk about these six theories about the monster. (A theory is an opinion.)
   a) It's salmon leaping around looking like a monster.
   b) It's a dragon or serpent that's been living in the loch for many years.
   c) It's a huge otter.
   d) It's a fake or fakes. (We do know that some pictures have been faked.)
   e) It's only rocks which can be seen when the water is low.
   f) It's a trick of the eye or camera which makes natural objects look like monsters.

3 For each theory make notes under these headings and be prepared to argue your case using your notes.

	Points for	Points against	Group's opinion
a.			
b.			

Other mysteries

On this page are a number of pictures.
Find out about the mysteries behind them.

Can he bend forks?
Who is he?
Do you believe it?
Find out more.

How did such a
large ship sink?
Find out more.

When did it happen?
Who killed the
President?
Find out more.

What are they?
Do they really exist?
What do you think?

Where is or was it?
Does it exist?
What do you think?

SATURDAY RADIO 30 August

1

MW 1053 +
1089 kHz
285 + 275 m
VHF/FM
88-90-2

VHF/FM Stereo between
1.0 pm and 7.30
News on the half hour until
12.30 pm, then 2.0, 3.30, 5.30,
7.30, 9.30, 12 midnight

6.0 am Mark Page
Producer TED BESTON

8.0 Peter Powell
Producer TED BESTON

10.0 Dave Lee Travis
Producer KEVIN HOWLETT

1.0 pm Adrian Juste
Producer ROGER PUSEY

3.0 The American Chart Show
America's latest hits and a
countdown of the US Top 40
direct from **New York**

with **Cleo Rowe**
Producer JOHN WALTERS

5.0 Saturday Live
Introduced by **Andy Kershaw**
Producer PHIL ROSS

6.30 In Concert
featuring **Chris Rea**
recorded at the Odeon,
Hammersmith, London
Introduced by **Pete Drummond**
Producer JEFF GRIFFIN
(R)

7.30 Simon Mayo
Saturday sounds and surprises
Producers LOUISE MUSGRAVE
and TED BESTON

9.30-12.0 ...unners Show

2

MW 693 +
909 kHz
433 +
330 M
VHF/FM
88-90-2

VHF/FM Stereo except
between 1.0 pm and 7.30
News on the hour until
1.0 pm then 3.0*, 6.0, 7.0
and hourly from 10.0
Headlines 6.30 am, 7.30
Major Bulletins 7.0 am, 8.0
and 12 midnight

Sport
Tennis: US Open
Reports at 11.2 pm, 12.5 am
Coverage also at 1.30 pm and
in desks at 11.2 am, 10.2 pm
Cricket Scoreboard 7.30 pm

4.0 am Dave Bussey
The Weekend Early Show
Group of the day: GENTLEMEN AND
PLAYERS WITH VOCAL REFRAIN
Producers MEL HOUSE
and COLIN CHANDLER

6.0 Steve Truelove
The Saturday Show
Producer DAVID WELSBY
BBC Birmingham

8.5 Angela Rippon
Producer KEN EVANS

10.0 Sounds of the 60s
Presented by **John Leyton**
including songs by BOB LUMAN,
THE FOUR SEASONS and
FRANK SINATRA
Producer IAN GRANT

11.0 Album Time
with **Peter Clayton**
Producer SANDRA BLACK
1.0 VHF/FM joins Radio 1

1.30 pm Sport on 2

Introduced by **Renton Laidlaw**
A specially extended edition
featuring the Marathon from
the **European Championships**,
football, cricket and US Open

1.0 pm Huddwinks
starring Roy Hudd
6: *Dead Men Don't Eat Pilchards*
(Broadcast last Thursday)

1.30 Sport on 2
see panel

NEW SERIES

6.30 Sports Quizkid
A home international quiz
**Peter Davies, Justin Welford
Ian Martin** and **Steven Wignall**
compete in the English heat
from **Cheadle High School,
Staffordshire.**
Questionmaster **Paul McDowell**
Producer HELEN GILL
● BACK PAGES: 78

7.0 Three in a Row
Stuart Hall presents the touring
general knowledge quiz from
**Bath College of Higher
Education.**
Questions set by DAVID WILLIAMS
Devised by DON DAVIS
Producer ANDY ALIFFE
7.30 VHF/FM rejoins Radio 2

**7.30 Rodgers and
Hammerstein at the Barbican**
starring **Lorna Dallas**
and **Willard White**
with **Mary Carewe, Michael Dore**
the **Stephen Hill Singers**
and the
BBC Concert Orchestra
conducted by **Stanley Black**
Highlights from *Oklahoma!*,
*Flower Drum Song, No Strings,
The King and I, Carousel,
State Fair, South Pacific*
and *The Sound of Music*
Introduced by **John Dunn**
Producer BARRY KNIGHT
*(First broadcast in March
in association with
Raymond Gubbay Ltd)*

8.20-8.40* Interval
Robert Cushman recalls
some memorable musical
opening nights.
(R)

competition at **Stuttgart.**
Football: commentary on the
second half of a top Football
League match, with regular
scores from around the
country and from the Premier
League in Scotland.
Cricket: *Britannic Assurance
County Championship*
With no championship match
today for Gloucestershire,
Essex have the opportunity to
take full advantage in the
chase for the title.
Scoreboards throughout
the programme.

5.0 Sports Report
The classified football results
and news information
...'s news of

1 Answer these questions about
   what was on the radio on
   Saturday, 30 August.
   a) What time does Radio 1
      come on the air?
   b) What is the only programme
      you could hear if you turned
      on the radio at 4.30 in the
      middle of the night?
   c) When does Dave Lee Travis
      finish his show?
   d) What country does Cleo
      Rowe play music from?
   e) At 10 pm on Radio 2 what
      decade of music is being
      played?
   f) When is Sport on 2?
   g) Who is the conductor for the
      BBC Concert Orchestra?
   h) Who introduces Album Time
      on Radio 2?

2 Write down the names of five
   Radio 1 disc jockeys.

3 Which three radio programmes
   would you choose to listen to?
   For each one give your reasons.

4 Make up questions based on
   this extract from *The Radio
   Times.*

5 Check this information about Monday evening's TV on ITV. For each statement, say if it is true or false.

a) *News at Ten* is preceded by *Central News*.
b) Central TV stops broadcasting at 12.05 am.
c) *ECO* is about wasting time in Sweden.
d) Coronation Street was written by Harry Kershaw.
e) Rita Fairclough is played by Barbara Knox.
f) The Krypton Factor is a Sci-fi film.
g) *Contact* looks at how handicapped people can develop their artistic talents.
h) *Murder with Mirrors* stars Bette Davis and Dorothy Tutin.
i) Agatha Christie wrote the screen play.
j) '*Not me pal*' is the second episode in a series.

6 Use a copy of last week's *Radio Times/TV Times* and make up your own questions.

Autumn ITV

Central

7.00

NEW SERIES
The Krypton Factor

GORDON BURNS

Television's toughest quiz returns for its 10th anniversary series with a fresh look and a new physical round — response. The famous assault course places demands on strength and stamina, but response provides a measure of physical fine-tuning through tests requiring manual dexterity, body flexibility and sharp reflexes. Six gruelling mental and physical rounds await the series' 48 contestants, all intent on becoming 'United Kingdom Superperson 1986' and winning the coveted *Krypton Factor* trophy. Plus, new this year, special trophies for the fastest man and woman over the assault course. Tonight's first-heat contestants are the Rev Jan Taylor, a clergyman from Belfast; Ruth Copping, a housewife from Shipley, Yorkshire; Liz Somerville, a design assistant from London; and Dexter Hutt, a teacher from Birmingham. Graphics by Murray Cook.

See page 23

Oracle subtitles page 888

RESEARCH ADELE EMM
DESIGNER NICK KING
DIRECTOR SPENCER CAMPBELL
PRODUCER GEOFF MOORE
EXECUTIVE PRODUCER
STEPHEN LEAHY
Granada Television Production

8.00

NEW SERIES
We'll Think of Something

BY GEOFF ROWLEY

SAM KELLY
MARCIA WARREN
'NOT ME PAL'

Start of a new six-part comedy series about Les Brooks, a middle-aged man learning to cope with unemployment — and refusing to let the system beat him.

See page 76

Les Brooks	Sam Kelly
Maureen Brooks	Marcia Warren
Dennis	Roger Sloman
Irene	Maggie Jones
Norman	Ray Mort
Eddie	Philip Dunbar
Dave	Jimmy Reddington
Old Mr Brooks	John Barrard
Doctor Khan	Tariq Yunus
Policeman	Ian Bleasdale

DESIGNER IAN RUSSELL
DIRECTOR/PRODUCER

7.30
Coronation Street

Alf Roberts finds out what it really means to be part of a family, while Mavis gets to grips with being 'the other woman'.

Oracle subtitles page 888

This week's cast:

Rita Fairclough	
Mavis Riley	Barbara Knox
Ivy Tilsley	Thelma Barlow
Brian Tilsley	Lynne Perrie
Vera Duckworth	Christopher Quinten
Mike Baldwin	Elizabeth Dawn
Susan Baldwin	Johnny Briggs
	Wendy Jane Walker
Terry Duckworth	Nigel Pivaro
Emily Bishop	Eileen Derbyshire
Alf Roberts	Bryan Mosley
Audrey Roberts	Sue Nicholls
Deirdre Barlow	Anne Kirkbride
Gail Tilsley	Helen Worth
Shirley Armitage	Lisa Lewis
Ida Clough	Helene Palmer
Derek Wilton	Peter Baldwin
Nicky Tilsley	Warren Jackson
Jenny Bradley	Sally Ann Matthews

WRITER H V KERSHAW
STORIES TOM ELLIOTT, PAUL ABBOTT
DESIGNER ERIC DEAKINS
EXECUTIVE PRODUCER
BILL PODMORE
DIRECTOR PEDR JAMES
PRODUCER JOHN G TEMPLE
Granada Television Production

8.30
Movie Premiere

HELEN HAYES
BETTE DAVIS
JOHN MILLS
LEO McKERN

AGATHA CHRISTIE'S MURDER WITH MIRRORS

FILM

Miss Jane Marple is asked to visit an old school friend, Carrie Louise, whose life, she comes to fear, may be in danger. At Carrie's palatial estate, Stonygates, on the outskirts of London, Miss Marple discovers that the property has been turned into a rehabilitation centre for several hundred juvenile delinquents.

See page 33

Miss Jane Marple	Helen Hayes
Carrie Louise	Bette Davis
Lewis Serrocold	John Mills
Insp Curry	Leo McKern
Gina	Liane Langland
Wally	John Laughlin
Mildred	Dorothy Tutin
Dr Max Hargrove	Anton Rodgers
Ms Bellever	Frances de la Tour
Christian Gulbrandsen	John Woodvine
Steven Restarick	James Coombes
Edgar	Tim Roth
Sgt Lake	Christopher Fairbank
Secretary	Amanda Maynard

TELEPLAY GEORGE ECKSTEIN
BASED ON THE NOVEL BY
AGATHA CHRISTIE
DIRECTOR DICK LOWRY

10.00 News at Ten

followed by

Central News

10.35 ECO

FIRES, PELLETS AND MUNCHING MICROBES

This week *ECO*, Central's environmental programme for the Midlands, looks at how we're wasting waste. Commentary is by Bob Hoskins. This year is Energy Efficiency Year but, sadly, British progress in this field is a long way behind that of countries like Sweden. *ECO* looks at brave initiatives in the Midlands

11.05
The Protectors

DECOY

BY BRIAN CLEMENS

A 'dead' man steps out of the past — bringing near-death for Harry and the Contessa.

Harry Rule	Robert Vaughn
Contessa	Nyree Dawn Porter
Paul Buchet	Tony Anholt
Lockier	Donald Houston
Devlin	Kenneth Colley

DIRECTOR CHARLES CRICHTON

11.35 Contact

Lee Corner of ARTLINK talks about a project which aims to encourage the artistic development of special groups in the community, ranging from handicapped toddlers in day nurseries to the elderly in residential care. ‡

RESEARCH BERNARD CARTWRIGHT,
LYNN TODD, DI STUBBS
PRODUCER/DIRECTOR
MICHAEL HART
Central Production

12.05am
Closedown

followed by

Central Jobfinder

Unit 12: Writing a story

Writing a story is like producing a book. There are many stages before the final version is completed.

1 The author has an idea and makes a plan.

2 The author finds out more information.

3 The author types out the manuscript.

4 The author takes it to the publisher.

5 The editor and author discuss possible improvements.

6 The author improves the original draft.

7 The editor checks the final version through and sends it to the printer.

8 The printer typesets the manuscript.

9 The editor and author correct any mistakes in the printing.

10 The designer pastes the typesetting on the pages and makes space for the pictures.

11 Artists and cartoonists draw the pictures.

12 The printer corrects any mistakes and adds in new material.

13 Any last-minute corrections are made.

14 The book is published about a year after the author finished writing it.

The stages of writing... The stages of writing...

Stage 1: Choosing

Deciding what to write about can be the most difficult stage.
Here are some popular kinds of stories.
Decide which one you would like to try, or think of one of your own.

Adventure A car chase A hi-jack	**Horror** The laughing ghost A terrible night
Mystery A murder case The story of the Loch Ness monster	**Fantasy** What you would do if . . . You in 20 years
Personal Your early years Your holiday	**Sci-fi** Aliens The year 2087

Here are some ways of getting started. Use them to help you begin.
a) Find a picture to help you.
b) Write down all your ideas on paper.
c) Think of the first and/or last sentence.
d) Make a list of all the people in your story.
e) Decide when and where your story happens.
f) Share ideas with a friend.
g) Read somebody else's story.
h) Try some different opening paragraphs.

Stage 2: Planning

Before you start writing your story make rough notes on:
a) what happens
b) the main scenes
c) the characters
d) the ending.

Stage 3: Writing a rough draft

You are now ready to write your story out for the first time.

Remember:
a) To use paragraphs. (Look back to pages 26–29 to remind yourself about paragraphs.)
b) Don't worry about mistakes at this stage.
c) Don't worry about what your writing looks like.

Stage 4: Improving your rough draft

Think carefully about what you have written. Can you make it better?
a) Get comments from a friend on your work.
b) Ask for advice from your teacher.

The stages of writing...

Stage 5: Writing a neat draft

Using the advice you have been given, make a neat version of your story.
a) Use a dictionary to check spellings.
b) Check sentences and paragraphs.
c) Improve weak parts of your story.
d) Add interesting words if you can.
e) Remove words that don't add anything.

Stage 6: Writing a final draft

After your teacher has checked your work, write up the final copy of your story.
a) Give it a title and date.
b) Add drawings if you want.

Stage 7: Feed-back and display

What do other people think of your story?
Your work is now ready to be marked, or commented on, or displayed, or made into a booklet.
a) Design a book cover for your story.
b) Design a poster for your story.

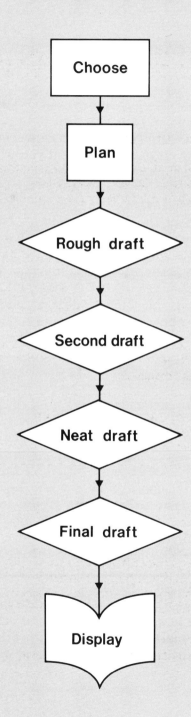

Lenny's red-letter day

by *Bernard Ashley*

Lenny Fraser is a boy in my class. Well, he's a boy in my class when he comes. But to tell the truth, he doesn't come very often. He stays away from school for a week at a time, and I'll tell you where he is. He's at the shops, stealing things sometimes, but mainly just opening the doors for people. He does it to keep himself warm. I've seen him in our shop. When he opens the door for someone, he stands around inside till he gets sent out. Of course, it's quite warm enough in school, but he hates coming. He's always got long, tangled hair, not very clean, and his clothes are too big or too small, and they call him 'Flea-bag'. He sits at a desk without a partner, and no one wants to hold his hand in games. All right, they're not to blame; but he isn't either. His mother never gets up in the morning, and his house is dirty. It's a house that everybody runs past very quickly.

But Lenny makes me laugh a lot. In the playground he's always saying funny things out of the corner of his mouth. He doesn't smile when he does it. He says these funny things as if he's complaining. For example, when Mr Cox the deputy head came to school in his new car, Lenny came too, that day; but he didn't join in all the admiration. He looked at the little car and said to me, 'Anyone missing a skateboard?'

He misses all the really good things, though – the School Journeys and the outing. And it was a big shame about his birthday.

It happens like this with birthdays in our class. Miss Blake lets everyone bring their cards and perhaps a small present to show the others. Then everyone sings 'Happy Birthday' and we give them bumps in the playground. If people can't bring a present, they tell everyone what they've got instead. I happen to know some people make up things that they've got just to be up with the others, but Miss Blake says it's good to share our Red-Letter Days.

I didn't know about these Red-Letter Days before. I thought they were something special in the post, like my dad handles in his Post Office in the shop. But Miss Blake told us they are red painted words in the prayer books, meaning special days.

Well, what I'm telling you is that Lenny came to school on his birthday this year. Of course, he didn't tell us it was his birthday, and, as it all worked out, it would have been better if Miss Blake hadn't noticed it in the register. But, 'How nice!' she said. 'Lenny's here on his birthday, and we can share it with him.'

It wasn't very nice for Lenny. He didn't have any cards to show the class, and he couldn't think of a birthday present to tell us about. He couldn't even think of anything funny to say out of the corner of his mouth. He just had to stand there looking foolish until Miss Blake started the singing of 'Happy Birthday' – and then half the people didn't bother to sing it. I felt very sorry for him, I tell you. But that wasn't the worst. The worst happened in the playground. I went to take his head end for bumps, and no one would come and take his feet. They all walked away. I had to finish up just patting him on the head with my hands, and before I knew what was coming out I was telling him, 'You can come home to tea with me, for your birthday.' And he said, yes, he would come.

My father works very hard in the Post Office, in a corner of our shop; and my mother stands at the door all day, where people pay for their groceries. When I get home from school, I carry cardboard boxes out to the yard and jump on them, or my big sister Nalini shows me which shelves to fill and I fill them with jam or chapatis – or birthday cards. On this day, though, I thought I'd use my key and go in through the side door and take Lenny straight upstairs – then hurry down again and tell my mum and dad that I'd got a friend in for an hour. I thought, I can get a birthday card and some cake and ice-cream from the shop, and Lenny can go home before they come upstairs. I wanted him to do that before my dad saw who it was, because he knows Lenny from his hanging around the shops.

Lenny said some funny things on the way home from school, but you know, I couldn't relax and enjoy them properly. I felt ashamed because I was wishing all the time that I hadn't asked him to come home with me. The bottoms of his trousers dragged along

the ground, he had no buttons on his shirt so the sleeves flapped, and his hair must have made it hard for him to see where he was going.

I was in luck because the shop was very busy. My dad had a queue of people to pay out, and my mum had a crowd at the till. I left Lenny in the living-room and I went down to get what I wanted from the shop. I found him a birthday card with a badge in it. When I came back, he was sitting in a chair and the television was switched on. He's a good one at helping himself, I thought. We watched some cartoons and then we played 'Monopoly', which Lenny had seen on the shelf. We had some crisps and cakes and lemonade while we were playing; but I had only one eye on my 'Monopoly' moves – the other eye was on the clock all the time. I was getting very impatient for the game to finish, because it looked as if Lenny would still be there when they came up from the shop. I did some really bad moves so that I could lose quickly, but it's very difficult to hurry up 'Monopoly', as you may know.

In the end I did such stupid things – like buying too many houses and selling Park Lane and Mayfair – that he won the game. He must have noticed what I was doing, but he didn't say anything to me. Hurriedly, I gave him his birthday card. He pretended not to take very much notice of it, but he put it in his shirt, and kept feeling it to make sure it was still there. At least, that's what I thought he was making sure about, there inside his shirt.

It was just the right time to say goodbye, and I'm just thinking he can go without anyone seeing him, when my sister came in. She had run up from the shop for something or other, and she put her head inside the room. At some other time, I would have laughed out loud at her stupid face. When she saw Lenny, she looked as if she'd opened the door and seen something really unpleasant. I could gladly have given her a good kick. She shut the door a lot quicker than she opened it, and I felt really bad about it.

'Nice to meet you,' Lenny joked, but his face said he wanted to go, too, and I wasn't going to be the one to stop him.

I let him out, and I heaved a big sigh. I felt good about being kind to him, the way you do when you've done a sponsored swim, and I'd done it without my mum and dad frowning at me about who I brought home. Only Nalini had seen him, and everyone knows she can make things seem worse than they are. I washed the glasses, and I can remember singing while I stood at the sink. I was feeling very pleased with myself.

My good feeling lasted about fifteen minutes; just long enough to be wearing off slightly. Then Nalini came in again and destroyed it altogether.

'Prakash, have you seen that envelope that was on the television top?' she asked. 'I put it on here when I came in from school.'

'No,' I said. It was very soon to be getting worried, but things inside me were turning over like clothes in a washing-machine. I knew already where all this was going to end up. 'What was in it?' My voice sounded to me as if it was coming from a great distance.

She was looking everywhere in the room, but she kept coming back to the television top as if the envelope would mysteriously appear there. She stood there now, staring at me. 'What was in it? What was in it was only a Postal Order for five pounds! Money for my school trip!'

'What does it look like?' I asked, but I think we both knew that I was only stalling. We both knew where it had gone.

'It's a white piece of paper in a brown envelope. It says "Postal Order" on it, in red.'

My washing-machine inside nearly went into a fast spin when I heard that. It was certainly Lenny's Red-Letter Day! But how could he be so ungrateful, I thought, when I was the only one to be kind to him? I clenched my fist while I pretended to look around. I wanted to punch him hard on the nose.

Then Nalini said what was in both our minds. 'It's that dirty kid who's got it. I'm going down to tell Dad. I don't know what makes you so stupid.'

Right at that moment I didn't know what made me so stupid, either, as to leave him up there on his own. I should have known. Didn't Miss Blake once say something about leopards never changing their spots?

When the shop closed, there was an awful business in the room. My dad was shouting-angry at me, and my mum couldn't think of anything good to say.

'You know where this boy lives,' my dad said. 'Tell me now, while I telephone the police. There's only one way of dealing with this sort of thing. If I go up there, I shall only get a mouthful of abuse. As if it isn't bad enough for you to see me losing things out of the shop, you have to bring untrustworthy people upstairs!'

My mum saw how unhappy I was, and she tried to make things better. 'Can't you cancel the Postal Order?' she asked him.

'Of course not. Even if he hasn't had the time to cash it somewhere else by now, how long do you think the Post Office would let me be Sub-Postmaster if I did that sort of thing?'

I was feeling very bad for all of us, but the thought of the police calling at Lenny's house was making me feel worse.

'I'll get it back,' I said. 'I'll go to his house. It's

only along the road from the school. And if I don't get it back, I can get the exact number of where he lives. *Then* you can telephone the police.' I had never spoken to my dad like that before, but I was feeling all shaky inside, and all the world seemed a different place to me that evening. I didn't give anybody a chance to argue with me. I ran straight out of the room and down to the street.

My secret hopes of seeing Lenny before I got to his house didn't come to anything. All too quickly I was there, pushing back his broken gate and walking up the cracked path to his front door. There wasn't a door knocker. I flapped the letter-box, and I started to think my dad was right. The police would have been better doing this than me.

I had never seen his mother before, only heard about her from other kids who lived near. When she opened the door, I could see she was a small lady with a tight mouth and eyes that said, 'Who are you?' and 'Go away from here!' at the same time.

She opened the door only a little bit, ready to slam it on me. I had to be quick.

'Is Lenny in, please?' I asked her.

She said, 'What's it to you?'

'He's a friend of mine,' I told her. 'Can I see him, please?'

She made a face as if she had something nasty in her mouth. '*Lenny!*' she shouted. '*Come here!*'

Lenny came slinking down the passage, like one of those scared animals in a circus. He kept his eyes on her hands, once he'd seen who it was at the door. There weren't any funny remarks coming from him.

She jerked her head at me. 'How many times have I told you not to bring kids to the house?' she shouted at him. She made it sound as if she was accusing him of a bad crime.

Lenny had nothing to say. She was hanging over him like a vulture about to fix its talons into a rabbit. It looked so out of place that it didn't seem real. Then it came to me that it could be play-acting – the two of them. He had given her the five pounds, and she was putting this on to get rid of me quickly.

But suddenly she slammed the door so hard in my face I could see how the glass in it came to be broken.

'Well, I don't want kids coming to my door!' she shouted at him on the other side. 'Breaking the gate, breaking the windows, wearing out the path. How can I keep this place nice when I'm forever dragging to the door?'

She hit him then, I know she did. There was no play-acting about the bang as a foot hit the door, and Lenny yelling out loud as if a desk lid had come down on his head. But I didn't stop to hear any more. I'd heard enough to turn my stomach sick.

Poor Lenny – I'd been worried about my mum and dad seeing him – and look what happened when his mother saw me! She had to be mad, that woman. And Lenny had to live with her! I didn't feel like crying, although my eyes had a hot rawness in them. More than anything, I just wanted to be back at home with my own family and the door shut tight.

Seeing my dad's car turn the corner was as if my dearest wish had been granted. He was going slowly, searching for me, with Nalini sitting up in front with big eyes. I waved, and ran to them. I got in the back and I drew in my breath to tell them to go straight home. It was worth fifty pounds not to have them knocking at Lenny's house, never mind five. But they were too busy trying to speak to me.

'Have you been to the house? Did you say anything?'

'Yes, I've been to the house, but –'

'Did you accuse him?'

'No. I didn't get a chance –'

They both sat back in their seats, as if the car would drive itself home.

'Well, we must be grateful for that.'

'We found the Postal Order.'

I could hardly believe what my ears were hearing. *They had found the Postal Order.* Lenny hadn't taken it, after all!

'It wasn't in its envelope,' Nalini was saying. 'He must have taken it out of that when he was tempted by it. But we can't accuse him of screwing up an envelope and hiding it in his pocket.'

'No, no,' I was saying, urging her to get on with things and tell me. 'So where was it?'

'In with the "Monopoly" money. He couldn't put it back on the television, so he must have kept it in his pile of "Monopoly" money, and put it back in the box.'

'Oh.'

'Mum found it. In all the commotion after you went out she knocked the box off the chair, and when she picked the bits up, there was the Postal Order.'

'It's certainly a good job you said nothing about it,' my dad said. 'And a good job I didn't telephone the police. We should have looked very small.'

All I could think was how small I had just felt, standing at Lenny's slammed door and hearing what his mother had said to him. And what about him getting beaten for having a friend call at his house?

My dad tried to be cheerful. 'Anyway, who won?' he asked.

'Lenny won the "Monopoly",' I said.

In bed that night, I lay awake a long time, thinking about it all. Lenny had taken some hard punishment from his mother. Some Red-Letter Day it had turned out to be! He would bear some hard thoughts about Prakash Patel.

He didn't come to school for a long time after that. But when he did, my heart sank into my boots. He came straight across the playground, the same flappy sleeves and dragging trouser bottoms, the same long, tangled hair – and he came straight for me. What would he do? Hit me? Spit in my face?

As he got close, I saw what was on his shirt, pinned there like a medal. It was his birthday badge.

'It's a good game, that "Monopoly",' he said out of the corner of his mouth. It was as if he was trying to tell me something.

'Yes,' I said. 'It's a good game all right.'

I hadn't got the guts to tell him that I'd gone straight home that night and thrown it in the dustbin. Dealings with houses didn't appeal to me any more.

Recording your progress in English:

Record Sheet 3

Name:				

Date of recording:	:)	:)	:)	

I can:				
write out speech in a story				
write simple instructions				
write a poem				
write out the alphabet				
improve my own writing				
plan a short story				
write the final draft of a story				
read simple instructions				
read poems				
read a script aloud				
find words in a dictionary				
read a whole short story				
listen to simple instructions				
give simple instructions				
argue a case				
talk about ideas for writing				
find books in a library				

Give your replies in the boxes below.
Make a separate list for number 5.

1. I am good at:

2. I think I have improved these skills:

3. I need more help with:

4 The activities I have enjoyed most in this book were:

5. I have read these books:
Title   Author   Content

Dictionary

A **accent** way of pronouncing words
address name of place where letters are directed
advertisement public notice, e.g. in newspaper or on television
announce make something known, say something publicly
answer speak in reply, often to a question
anxious nervous, troubled, uneasy
appalled shocked, dismayed, horrified
assure tell confidently, confirm, convince

B **berserk** mad, furious, wild
blank empty, not filled in
blaze flame, fire
Botanic garden place where plants are grown and studied
briskly quickly

C **castor-oil** oil used as medicine
confident sure, positive about self
conservatory room like a green-house
curator person in charge, keeper, manager

D **depot** base camp
determined with your mind firmly made up
draft stage of writing

E **emergency** sudden dangerous event
enquire ask a question
excessive too much or too great
experience thing that happens to a person, knowledge picked up from something happening to a person
extract small part of a book or piece of writing

F **fake** something made to look real so as to deceive people

G **gallery** place where pictures are hung in a house or museum
grimly severely, sternly, strictly
guilty found to have done something wrong, feeling that you have done wrong

H **hastily** rapidly, done too quickly
hitch-hiker someone who travels by being given lifts
hypnotised put into a condition like deep sleep

I **illegal** against the law, not legal

J **jagged** not straight, uneven and sharp

K

L **location** place where something is
loiter be slow in moving, hang about

M **malfunction** work badly or stop working
mango fruit
matted tangled
mosque Muslim place of worship

N **nationality** quality of being from a particular nation or country, e.g. Scottish or Indian.
neatly tidily, cleanly, smartly

O **obstinately** stubbornly

P **patience** 1 being patient, 2 a card game for one person
pause short stop, break or gap
precinct part of a city or town where traffic is not allowed
prey animal hunted and killed by another animal
prohibited forbidden, not allowed
prospect possibility, hope, life ahead
putty soft paste which sets hard, used in fixing windows

Q **questionnaire** series of questions normally on a particular subject
queue line of people or things waiting in order

R **receiver** part of the telephone used for listening
record describe things that have happened
refined polished, polite, elegant, not rude or crude
reply answer

S **satellite** kind of spacecraft that moves in orbit round a planet
scream cry out loudly
script the words of a play written down
sentry soldier on guard
shout speak in a loud voice
similar like
sniffle sniff quietly sometimes when crying
sternly strongly, firmly
storey floor of a house or flat
stranger somebody you do not know
strap strip of leather used for beating
surf waves as they break on the shore or beach

T **talkative** chatty, given to talk, wordy
temptation state of being encouraged to do something wrong

U **utensil** something used for a task, e.g. knife, fork

V **vanish** disappear

W **widow** woman whose husband has died

X

Y **yeast** substance used in making bread and beer

Z

Answers

A Alphabets (page 106).
a) = Greek; **b)** = Hindi; **c)** = Arabic; **d)** = Russian.

Acknowledgements

The publishers wish to thank the following for permission to use copyright material:

Affor: *Talking Blues*, Affor, Birmingham **Bernard Ashley:** "Lenny's Red-Letter Day" from *I'm Trying To Tell You* (Kestrel Books, 1981), copyright © 1981 by Bernard Ashley. Reprinted by permission of Penguin Books Ltd. **Pip & Jane Baker:** extract from a Dr. Who script, "The Mark of the Rani", © 1984. Reprinted by permission of the authors. **Sabir Bandali:** 'Small Accidents' from *Our Lives* (ILEA English Centre). Used with permission. **Stan Barstow:** from *Joby*. Reprinted by permission of Michael Joseph Ltd. **Nina Bawden:** from *Kept in the Dark*. Reprinted by permission of Victor Golancz Ltd. **Peter Benchley:** adapted from *Jaws*. Reprinted by permission of Century Hutchinson Publishing Group Ltd. **Betsy Byars:** from *The Pinballs* (1977). Reproduced by permission of The Bodley Head. **Victor Canning:** from *The Runaways*. Reprinted by permission of William Heinemann. **Peter Carter:** from *Under Goliath* (1977). Reprinted by permission of Oxford University Press. **J. Charlesworth & T. Brown:** from the play *Tom Sawyer* (1976). Reprinted by permission of Heinemann Educational Ltd. **Apsley Cherry-Garrard:** adapted from "A Diary of Courage", in *The Worst Journey in the World*, Vol. 2 (1937). Reprinted by permission of the author's estate and Chatto & Windus. **Beverley Cleary:** from *Fifteen* (Penguin Books, Ltd). Reprinted by permission of Laurence Pollinger Ltd. **Farrukh Dhondy:** "Free Dinners" from *Come to Mecca and Other Stories* (Fontana Lions, 1978). Reprinted by permission of Collins Publishers. **Janet Frame:** from *To The-Island* (Women's Press Ltd.). **Mick Gower:** "Christmas Thank you's" from *Swings and Roundabouts*. Reprinted by permission of Collins Publishers. **S. E. Hinton:** from *The Outsiders*. Reprinted by permission of Victor Gollancz Ltd. **Roderic Jefferies:** from *Eighteen Desperate Hours* (1979). Reprinted by permission of Hodder & Stoughton Ltd. **Linton Kwesi Johnson:** "Sonny's Lettah" from *Inglan Is A Bitch* (Race Today Publications). Used by permission of the publisher. **Gene Kemp:** from *No Place Like*. Reprinted by permission of Faber & Faber Ltd. **Clive King:** from *Stig of the Dump* (Puffin Books). Reprinted by permission of Murray Pollinger, Literary Agent. **Zohra El Kssmi:** 'Families' from *Our Lives* (ILEA, English Centre). Used with permission. **George Layton:** from *A Northern Childhood: The Fib & Other Stories* (Knockouts Series, Longman Group Ltd., 1978). Used by permission of the publisher. **Julius Lester:** from *Long Journey Home* (Longman Young Books, 1973), copyright © Julius Lester, 1972. Reprinted by permission of Penguin Books Ltd. **Roger McGough:** "Watchwords" from *Watchwords* (Jonathan Cape Ltd). Reprinted by permission of A. D. Peters & Co., Ltd. **Errol O'Connor:** from *Jamaica Child*, (ILEA, English Centre). Used with permission. **Peckham Publishing Project:** "How to make fish tea" from *Milk River: An Anthology of West Indian Writing*. **Michael Rosen:** "Mart was my best friend" Reprinted by permission of Andre Deutsch Ltd. **Sylvia Sherry:** from *A Pair of Jesus Boots*, dramatised by Alan England. Reprinted by permission of Heinemann Educational Books Ltd. **James P. Taylor:** from *How To Catch a Dragon* (Edward Arnold, 1981), adapted from Walter Stolle *The World Beneath My Bicycle Wheel* published by Pelham Books. Used with permission. **Sue Townsend:** from *The Secret Diary of Adrian Mole Aged 13¾*. Reprinted by permission of Methuen London. **Demetroulla Vassili:** "Don't Interrupt" from *City Lines* (ILEA, English Centre, 1982). Used with permission. **Robert Westall:** from *The Machine-Gunners*. Reprinted by permission of Macmillan, London & Basingstoke.

Every effort has been made to trace copyright holders but sometimes without success. We shall be pleased to rectify any omissions at the first imprint if copyright holders will contact us.

The publishers wish to thank the following for permission to use photographic material:

Aerofilms p.69 (top left); Andes Press Agency p.30; Barnaby's Picture Library pp.9, 68 (bottom), 69 (top right), 84, 94 (top); BBC Enterprises p.49; J. Allan Cash pp.17 (bottom left), 41 (right), 54 (bottom centre), 69 (bottom right and left); Format Photographers/Pam Isherwood pp.47 (centre left and right),/Maggie Murray 41 (top),/Raissa Page 47 (top and bottom left), 54 (top right), 54 (top centre),/Brenda Prince 54 (bottom left); Fortean Picture Library pp.112, 113 (top left); Rob Judges pp.37, 41 (bottom), 50, 52, 57, 67, 72 (all), 73 (all), 92; London Regional Transport p.91; Charles Barker Lyons Ltd. p.17 (bottom right); Mary Evans Picture Library p.113 (top centre); Network Photographers/Martin Mayer pp.47 (bottom right),/Mike Abrahams 94 (centre); The Photo Source pp.111, 113 (top right and bottom right); Mark Rosser p.17 (top right); Thomson Holidays p.17 (top left).

The illustrations are by Rupert Besley, Judy Brown, Helen Clipson, John Cooper, Allan Curless, Peter Elson, John James, Peter Joyce, Alan Marks, John Ridgway, Ursula Sieger, Barrie Thorpe, Shaun Williams, and Farida Zaman.